School Administrators and Technology

Meeting the Standards

Bridget M. Connor
Danea A. Farley
Gregory A. Wise

UNIVERSITY PRESS OF AMERICA,® INC.
Lanham • Boulder • New York • Toronto • Plymouth, UK

Copyright © 2010 by
University Press of America,® Inc.
4501 Forbes Boulevard
Suite 200
Lanham, Maryland 20706
UPA Acquisitions Department (301) 459-3366
Estover Road
Plymouth PL6 7PY
United Kingdom
All rights reserved
Printed in the United States of America
British Library Cataloging in Publication Information Available
Library of Congress Control Number: 2010920126
ISBN: 978-0-7618-5072-4 (paperback : alk. paper)
eISBN: 978-0-7618-5073-1

∞™ The paper used in this publication meets the minimum requirements of American National Standard for Information Sciences—Permanence of Paper for Printed Library Materials, ANSI/NISO Z39.48-1992.

For
Kathleen Marie Engers, SSND
John S. Harrison
Michael Pitroff

Contents

List of Tables	vii
Acknowledgments	ix
Introduction	xi

1 Infrastructure and Instruction: Right Resources, Right People — 1

- Introduction — 1
  - Infrastructure: Right Resources — 1
  - Educational Administrators — 2
- Activities — 2
  - Background Information and Interviews — 2
  - Technology Management Systems — 3
  - Budgetary Considerations — 3
  - Existing Systems and Strategies for Improvement — 7
- Instruction: Right People — 7
- Activities — 8
  - Using Data to Improve Student Achievement — 8
  - Faculty Professional Development — 15

2 Leading with a Shared Vision — 25

- Introduction — 25
  - Educational Administrators — 25
- Activities — 26
  - 1. Data Analysis of Faculty Professional Growth Needs — 26
  - 2. Faculty Technology Professional Growth Plan and Timeline — 26
  - 3. Advocating Technology — 28

3	Navigating the Digital Culture: Social, Legal and Ethical Issues	34
	Introduction	34
	Activities	35
	1. Reflection on Present Knowledge	35
	2. Internet Search	35
	3. Social, Legal Ethical Search Log	36
	4. Informal Scenario Review	38
	5. Case Study and Observations: Technology Issues in the Educational Setting	39
4	Technology and Its Impact on Professional Practice	46
	Introduction	46
	Activities	47
	1. Technology Resources Summary	47
	2. Personal Assessment	48
	3. Faculty Interviews	48
	4. Summarize the Data from the Faculty Surveys	48
	5. Student Interviews	49
	6. Student Input	49
	7. Social, Legal Ethical Summary	50
	8. PowerPoint Presentation	50
	Chapter End Reflection Questions	51
5	Learning and Teaching	54
	Introduction	54
	Activities	55
	1. Technology Enriched Lesson Plan Preliminary Preparation	55
	2. Lesson Presentation	58
	3. Summary of Peer Feedback	58
	Index	67

Tables

1.1.	Technology Interviews and Budget Narrative	4
1.2.	Technology Interviews and Budget Narrative Scoring Tool	5
1.3.	Class Grade Book	10
1.4.	Additional Data	12
1.5.	Using Data to Improve Student Achievement Data Analysis and Instructional Decisions	14
1.6.	Using Data to Improve Student Achievement Scoring Tool	16
1.7.	Using Data Professional Development Outline	20
1.8.	Using Data Professional Development Outline Scoring Tool	21
1.9.	Faculty Technology Professional Growth Plan Checklist	23
1.10.	Faculty Technology Professional Growth Plan Checklist Data Analysis	24
2.1.	Faculty Technology Professional Growth Plan Timeline	29
2.2.	Potential Opportunities for Advocacy	31
2.3.	Faculty Technology Professional Growth Plan Technology and Timeline Potential Scoring Tool	32
3.1.	Search Log Scoring Tool	37
3.2.	Case Study and Observation/Reflection Scoring Tool	43
4.1.	Social, Legal, and Ethical Uses of Technology PowerPoint Presentation Scoring Tool	52
5.1.	Technology Enriched Lesson Plan Proposal for a One-Day Lesson	56
5.2.	Technology Enriched Lesson Plan Format	59
5.3.	Technology Enriched Lesson Plan Peer Feedback	61
5.4.	Technology Enriched Lesson Plan Scoring Tool	63

Acknowledgments

The authors would like to express their thanks to the International Society for Technology in Education (ISTE) for permission to reference the NETS for Administrators: National Technology Standards for Administrators, ©2009, ISTE ®; to Baltimore County (Maryland) Public Schools' Office of Information Technology for permission to modify their *Technology Lesson Look Fors* for inclusion in this book; and for permission to develop materials from those designed through Maryland's *Preparing Tomorrow's Teachers to Use Technology* (PT3), USDOE Catalyst Grant P342A990201, May 2002.

Introduction

Administrator, teacher, and student performance have long been measured against established standards. Competency in identified areas of expertise not only assures a level of individual administrator proficiency, but also can be instrumental in bringing the school program and goals into alignment with school system or district goals. As instructional leaders, school administrators are critical to the formulation of a school wide plan for technology implementation. They are responsible for:

- focusing on systemic improvement
- formulating a shared vision for the school with input from teaching colleagues
- fulfilling professional development needs
- maintaining and providing access to digital tools and resources that support teaching and learning and daily operations and management
- establishing and promoting policies for the use of these resources
- maximizing communication, collaboration, growth, and purposeful change
- encouraging innovation and creativity

How can a classroom teacher, who desires to contribute to the field of education as a school administrator, acquire the necessary skills and understandings to promote the excellence that can transform a school organization? How can the guidance of technology standards assist in this acquisition?

First, it is critical to identify standards that are internationally recognized. The technology standards for administrators (NETS-A), established in 2009 by the International Society for Technology in Education (ISTE), is just such a set of standards. Each standard includes specific performance indicators, which all activities in this workbook are designed to measure.

The activities themselves were developed with the spectrum of classroom teacher technology experience as a backdrop. This was done not only to validate the technology skills teachers bring to the administrator role, but also to maintain a deep awareness of their perspective. A conscious effort was made to address practicality, student choice, access to resources, and above all, a wide variety of tasks and products. To successfully complete these activities, students will want to have access to the Internet and Microsoft Office®, specifically Word®, Excel®, and PowerPoint®.

Whether giving students flexibility in choosing activities or using this workbook as part of a highly structured course for prospective administrators, it is recommended that instructors encourage students to progress in chapter order. Certain tasks in early chapters are used as foundational material for subsequent activities. The templates found in various tables throughout the workbook are available in electronic format by contacting any of the authors via email: Sister Bridget Connor, GNSH at bconnor@ndm.edu; Danea A. Farley at dfarley@ndm.edu; or Gregory A. Wise at gwise@ndm.edu. A scoring tool is provided in each chapter for each key task or product.

Chapter One

Infrastructure and Instruction: Right Resources, Right People

INTRODUCTION

The role of the school administrator has evolved into a multifaceted one that has expanded beyond curriculum, teachers, students, and parents. Administrators must exhibit both managerial and instructional leadership. In order for schools to sustain systemic improvement, administrators must harness the available technological tools to manage resources. This enables faculty and staff to provide a learning culture in which data is used effectively to guide all aspects of school operation and to plan for future needs. Competent teachers are hired and equipped with appropriate professional development to deliver an engaging curriculum in a technologically-rich learning environment. Students reach their learning goals.

Infrastructure: Right Resources

Without question, technology can be a powerful educational tool. But with it comes a host of new issues:

- What is the school's vision for technology use by all stakeholders?
- What is the best equipment for a school to have to meet the needs of its students?
- How will funding for needed equipment be secured?
- Who is going to maintain equipment?
- Who is going to control a school or school system's networks and access to that network so that students are safe?
- When and how should equipment be replaced?

These and many more questions will demand answers, if there is going to be a successful integration of technology into educational programs. These issues fall squarely on the shoulders of school administrators, and become agenda items to address.

The National Technology Standard that promotes systemic improvement is Standard IV. Educational Administrators provide digital-age leadership and management to improve the organization continuously through the effective use of information and technology resources.

Educational Administrators

a. lead purposeful change to maximize the achievement of learning goals through the appropriate use of technology and media-rich resources
b. collaborate to establish metrics, collect and analyze data, interpret results, and share findings to improve staff performance and student learning
c. recruit and retain highly competent personnel who use technology creatively and proficiently to advance academic and operational goals
d. establish and leverage strategic partnerships to support systemic improvement
e. establish and maintain a robust infrastructure for technology including integrated, interoperable technology systems to support management, operations, teaching, and learning

Activities in this chapter that relate to providing and maintaining school technology infrastructure include:

1. Reading an article for background knowledge and then conducting an interview with school administrators regarding technology compatibility issues
2. Identification of technological management systems already in use
3. Review of a school or district technology budget and make recommendations regarding the technology budgetary process
4. Describing existing technology systems in your school and suggesting ways that those systems could be improved
5. Proposing a timeline for on-going evaluation and improvement of technology systems

Table 1.2 Technology Interviews and Budget Narrative Scoring Tool has been included to guide your work.

ACTIVITIES

Background Information and Interviews

Read an article on school funding for technology, such as "Providing the Basics: A Computer That Works" by Robert J. Gravina from *The School Administrator* at http://www.aasa.org/publications/saarticledetail.cfm?ItemNumber=8219&snItemNumber=950. This article comes from a publication with which school administrators should become familiar. As the article indicates, identifying funding resources and keeping up with the many and constant technological changes can be a school administrator's nemesis. As a future administrator, you should know what your school or school system's policies are regarding the purchase and use of technology. Interview two of the following persons:

- an administrator who is in charge of facilities
- an administrator who is in charge of budget allocations
- the technology coordinator, library media specialist, or other personnel in charge of technology decisions/input

Then, using the appropriate section of Table 1.1 Technology Interviews and Budget Narrative, write a narrative describing the interviewees' answers to the following questions and your reactions to their responses:

- What is your school or school district's policy regarding the purchase of hardware? What guidelines exist regarding purchases? Are specific vendors identified? How is the hardware paid for and by whom? Are there limits, restrictions, or other guidelines on what can be purchased? Who is responsible for ensuring technological compatibility of equipment?
- What is your school or school district's policy regarding the evaluation and purchase of software? Are schools limited in what they can purchase and from whom? Who is responsible for maintaining licenses and observing copyright laws?
- Are school staff members consulted regarding the use of hardware and software? What is presented to the staff regarding these issues? Is the interviewee aware of any frustrations the school staff may experience regarding such issues?

At the conclusion of your interview, what did you see as the school's strengths and weaknesses regarding hardware and software issues?

Technology Management Systems

Use the "Technology Management Systems" portion of Table 1.1 Technology Interviews and Budget Narrative to describe the administrative and instructional software products currently used at your school or a school that you know well, if you are not currently teaching. Include grade book, student information, budgetary, school scheduling, productivity (Microsoft Office, etc.), instructional, and other kinds of software. Add rows to the table as needed to create a complete list.

Budgetary Considerations

Look at your school or school system's technology budget. You may be able to find your system's budget online at their web site. If you can't find any other budget, the Ithaca, NY, school system's budget can be found at http://www.icsd.k12.ny.us/board/budget/2006-07/2006-2007BudgetBackground-IIT.pdf. It is fairly typical of most school system's technology budgets. Can you notice any particular foci in the budgets you see? Write a brief narrative describing what is indicated by the budgetary figures. What suggestions would you offer concerning these budgets? Justify your suggestions. Reflect on the level of support for technology that your school or school system provides.

Table 1.1. Technology Interviews and Budget Narrative

Interview Narrative					
Technology Management Systems					
Software Product	Used by (persons)	Used for (purpose)	Users' reactions to the product	How does this product meet its intended needs?	How do users feel the products could be improved?
Budgetary Concerns Narrative					
Reflection On a scale of 1 to 10, with 10 being full support and 1 being general lack of support, where do you rank your school or school system? Explain your ranking.					
Existing Systems and Strategies for Improvement Narrative					

	Timeline for Ongoing Evaluation and Improvement of Technology Systems		
	Year 1 (20)	Year 2 (20)	Year 3 (20)
Hardware purchase and replacement (Anticipate the school's needs.)			
Software purchase (Are there new products to be purchased or old ones upgraded?)			
Professional development for hardware and/or software			
Staffing Needs (to maintain and repair equipment and to provide training)			
Funding Sources			

Table 1.2. Technology Interviews and Budget Narrative Scoring Tool

Criterion	Unacceptable (1)	Acceptable (2)	Competent (3)	Exemplary (4)
Interviews	One interview was conducted but was not thorough or in-depth. Policies and guidelines to ensure technological equipment compatibility are described but could be more detailed and comprehensive.	One interview was conducted and was thorough and in-depth Policies and guidelines to ensure technological equipment compatibility are described but could be more detailed, or comprehensive.	Two interviews were conducted, but could have been more thorough and in-depth. Policies and guidelines to ensure technological equipment compatibility are described in a somewhat superficial way.	Two interviews were thorough and in-depth and policies and description of guidelines to ensure technological equipment compatibility are detailed and comprehensible.
Technology-based Management and Operations Systems in Schools	Few school uses of technology-based management and operations procedures were listed and could have been described in better detail.	Some school uses of technology-based management and operations procedures were listed but could have been described in better detail.	Some school uses of technology-based management and operations procedures were listed and described in good detail.	Many school uses of technology-based management and operations procedures were listed and described in good detail.
Resources to Complete and Sustain Technological Programs in Schools	A district or school technology budget was not adequately described and/or suggestions were not made and justified adequately regarding a budget focus on instructional technology needs.	A district or school technology budget is described in minimal detail and some suggestions were made and justified regarding a budget focus on instructional technology needs.	A district or school technology budget is described in good detail and some suggestions were made and justified regarding a budget focus on instructional technology needs.	A district or school technology budget is described in good detail and many suggestions were made and justified regarding a budget focus on instructional technology needs.

(continued)

Table 1.2. (continued)

Criterion	Unacceptable (1)	Acceptable (2)	Competent (3)	Exemplary (4)
Narrative regarding Existing Facilities and Staff Development Programs and Strategies for their Improvement, including Proposed Timeline for Evaluation and Improvement of Technology Systems	The narrative fails to outline the existing facilities and training opportunities at a school and/or fails to propose strategies to improve the current facilities, staff development, etc., regarding instructional technology.	The narrative outlines in minimal detail the existing facilities and training opportunities at a school and then goes on to minimally propose strategies to improve the current facilities, staff development, etc., regarding instructional technology.	The narrative outlines in minimal detail the existing facilities and training opportunities at a school but then goes on to adequately propose strategies to improve the current facilities, staff development, etc., regarding instructional technology.	The narrative outlines in great detail the existing facilities and training opportunities at a school and then goes on to propose many strategies to improve further the current facilities, staff development, etc., regarding instructional technology.
	A timeline is not provided.	A timeline is provided but guidelines for on-going evaluation or improvement of technology systems may be missing.	A timeline is provided which includes minimal guidelines for on-going evaluation and improvement of technology systems.	A detailed timeline is provided for on-going evaluation and improvement of technology systems.
Timeline for on-going evaluation and improvement of technology systems.	The timeline fails to address issues that would be important to evaluate and improve the technological systems of a school.	The timeline is not very full and addresses only a few issues that would be important to evaluate and improve the technological systems of a school.	The timeline is somewhat full and addresses many issues that would be important to evaluate and improve the technological systems of a school.	The timeline is full and addresses most issues that would be important to evaluate and improve the technological systems of a school.

Existing Systems and Strategies for Improvement

Looking specifically at school or school system management software, collect information regarding programs used by your school or school system for student information management, budgetary processes, school scheduling, facilities issues, etc. (You will have done some of this in Activity 3 above). Focusing only on these school or school system management software products, ask those using and administering these programs in your school the following questions:

- How were these software products chosen for your school?
- What kind of training are new users given on the various products?
- Do classroom teachers have access to any of these systems? Who on the school staff has access to these products?
- Do your students' parents have access to any part of these systems, i.e. grades, teacher web pages, etc.?
- What strengths and weaknesses do various staff members identify regarding the different products? How would they like to see them improved?

Using the appropriate section of Table 1.1 Technology Interviews and Budget Narrative, write a brief narrative describing your findings.

As you've probably seen by now, establishing and maintaining the needed technological assets for a school is a daunting task, but one with which school administrators often find themselves confronted. They must not only be up-to-date regarding the newest products, but work to find funding to provide those products and replace outdated or broken equipment. They also need to provide training for their staff and staff members to support all of these programs. Use the appropriate section of Table 1.1 to create a three-year plan for your school regarding various technological components school administrators would need to address. Make brief comments regarding what will need to take place during each year over a three-year period for each component.

INSTRUCTION: RIGHT PEOPLE

Successful leaders make informed decisions on the basis of sound research, using the wide variety of information available to them. They use data to guide decision-making. As regards technology, they use multiple methods to collect, assess, and analyze data, interpret the results, and communicate their findings in order to improve existing practice. As members of the administrative team, they devise a comprehensive plan that addresses the technology needed for the smooth operation of the school. They craft responses to the technology professional development needs of the faculty in order to improve instructional practice and student learning. In collaboration with the faculty, they devise a professional growth plan in order to identify those with expertise in technology, as well as to encourage and develop future leaders through involvement in advocacy opportunities. Effective leaders recruit, retain, and provide needed professional growth opportunities in order for good teaching to lead to the achievement of learning goals. By fostering a systematic and forward-looking approach to the use of data in all aspects of school operation, administrators can themselves make, as well as encourage staff to make, data-driven decisions at all levels and thereby, meet the instructional needs of the students. Sharing the data and collaborating on solutions and on a plan for implementation and re-evaluation derived from the data, empower all stakeholders in a partnership for improvement.

Activities in this chapter that relate to the use of data for instructional improvement include:

1. Using a Sample Excel® Grade Book (electronic version available via email by contacting one of the authors) to calculate averages, sort data, and graph results
2. Performing data analysis, data interpretation, reporting of findings, and the development of instructional solutions that address established school improvement goals based on the Sample Excel Grade Book data
3. Administration, analysis, and summary of findings from the Faculty Technology Professional Growth Checklist
4. Development of a faculty Professional Development Activity on data analysis for instructional decision-making (similar to Activities 1 and 2 above) which should be included in the Faculty Technology Professional Growth Plan timeline in Chapter 2.

ACTIVITIES

Using Data to Improve Student Achievement

Administrators are guided in their decision-making by the findings derived from the data available to them. They foster the use of data to encourage systemic improvement. In the area of instruction, the use of data to improve student achievement is critical. Administrators assume a key role in helping teachers to analyze student data, develop findings from that data, and then make instructional decisions that impact student achievement. In order to prepare for the administrator's role in this process, it is helpful to examine the process from the perspective of the individual teacher. Activities 1 and 2 provide just such an examination.

1. Preparing for a team meeting

Assume that you are a classroom teacher preparing for a grade level or content area team meeting. The purpose of the meeting is to discuss student and class performance during the first six weeks of school relative to the school improvement plan goals that your faculty set at the beginning of the school year. Your school improvement plan includes achieving the following three school goals for student performance:

- Each student will achieve a score of 7 out of 10 on each assessment of each of three targeted objectives from the Voluntary State Curriculum.

- Each student will achieve a score of at least 4 out of 5 for homework completion and accuracy on a scale of 1–5, where a 5 indicates that homework is always complete and accurate.
- Each student will have at least a 95% school attendance rate.

To provide an authentic context for the data, you will select three related objectives from your content area curriculum to pair with each of the three sets of assessment data.

Table 1.3—Class Grade Book contains performance data for your class of 25 students. The students' scores reflect their performance on one standard and three related goals/objectives, which you will select, for a selected content area. Each week, for each goal/objective addressed, students completed a variety of assessments. The total point value of each assessment was 10. The data in the table represents five assessment scores for each of the three goals/objectives. The Class Grade Book also includes attendance data and an overall average score for homework assignments for this period. In the electronic version of the Class Grade Book spreadsheet, Table 1.4—Additional Data can be found on a second tab at the bottom of the Class Grade Book. Table 1.4 contains additional information on the same 25 students, including whether each student has been classified as an English Language Learner (ELL) or as a Special Education student with an Individual Educational Plan (IEP). Table 1.4 also includes student scores on the Reading and Math portions of a state school assessment.

As you analyze the data in the Class Grade Book, you will make observations and instructional decisions for individual students and groups in your class. Please note that, for the purpose of this task, the type of data provided has been limited. In an actual school setting, data collection will also include non-numeric assessments to provide a complete evaluation of student performance.

Complete the following in preparation for your grade level or content area meeting:

a. My Grade Book Spreadsheet:

Before you begin, access the electronic version of the grade book in Excel®. Save the Class Grade Book under your last name and add the words "My Grade Book" (e.g. Smith My Grade Book). Using the renamed "(Your Last Name) My Grade Book," select a content area and fill in a standard and three related goals/objectives for your class. Select these from your content area curriculum. As an example, you will find the Maryland Voluntary State Curriculum, at http://www.mdk12.org.

b. Individual and Class Averages:

Using the grade book, calculate the individual and class average score for each of the three objectives on "(Your Last Name) My Grade Book." Report each average to one decimal place. Calculate the class average for homework and attendance performance. Report each average to one decimal place.

c. My Sorted Grade Book

Using the grade book, sort the average student performance on Goal/Objective 3 in descending order.

Table 1.3. Class Grade Book

1st Six Weeks	Standard:																			Attendance	Homework
	Goal/Objective # 1:						Goal/Objective # 2:						Goal/Objective # 3:								1-5 (5 –complete)
Student:	1	2	3	4	5	AVG	1	2	3	4	5	AVG	1	2	3	4	5	AVG		
1	8	8	6	7	7		6	6	5	6	5		3	4	3	3	4		93	3
2	4	5	5	5	4		3	4	2	2	2		2	3	4	3	5		80	3
3	3	2	4	4	5		5	6	4	5	3		4	3	4	4	4		86	2
4	7	7	8	9	10		7	8	9	8	7		6	8	7	8	9		90	4
5	8	9	9	9	10		6	8	7	8	9		7	7	8	9	9		100	5
6	5	5	6	7	7		2	3	4	3	4		4	4	3	3	3		78	1
7	3	3	2	3	2		4	6	4	5	3		4	4	5	5	5		87	2
8	7	7	7	8	7		9	5	7	7	6		7	8	7	7	8		78	4
9	9	10	8	9	10		7	8	7	7	7		7	7	7	6	8		96	5
10	5	4	6	5	4		3	5	4	5	4		3	3	4	3	2		92	4
11	6	7	7	7	7		7	8	7	9	9		7	8	9	10	10		94	4
12	7	8	8	7	8		7	8	5	9	7		8	8	8	8	7		82	4
13	5	6	6	7	5		3	4	3	4	4		2	3	2	1	2		98	4
14	6	5	7	5	6		4	4	4	5	5		4	3	4	4	4		81	1
15	5	6	7	7	7		4	5	4	4	4		3	2	3	2	2		68	0
16	9	9	10	9	10		7	8	8	9	10		7	6	8	7	7		84	4

Infrastructure and Instruction: Right Resources, Right People 11

1st Six Weeks	Standard:																			Attendance	Homework
	Goal/Objective #1:						Goal/Objective #2:						Goal/Objective #3:								1-5 (5 –complete)
Student:	1	2	3	4	5	AVG	1	2	3	4	5	AVG	1	2	3	4	5	AVG			
17	8	9	9	8	8		7	8	8	9	9		7	7	6	7	7			100	5
18	8	8	8	9	9		7	8	7	9	9		7	8	7	6	7			92	4
19	9	10	10	9	10		7	6	7	9	8		7	6	5	5	6			94	4
20	7	7	8	8	8		4	6	7	5	7		7	8	7	7	7			94	4
21	2	2	3	3	3		2	4	5	3	3		2	2	4	5	4			65	1
22	3	4	4	5	4		6	5	7	5	4		4	2	2	2	2			64	0
23	0	1	0	1	0		2	2	2	2	2		2	2	2	2	3			98	4
24	0	1	0	0	1		1	2	2	1	2		0	0	1	0	1			99	5
25	4	4	5	5	5		3	5	7	5	4		5	5	4	4	4			100	4
CLASS AVE																					

Table 1.4. Additional Data

Students	*ELL	**State Reading	**State Math	***IEP
1	N	P	P	N
2	N	B	B	Y
3	Y	B	B	N
4	N	A	A	N
5	N	A	A	N
6	N	P	B	Y
7	Y	B	P	N
8	N	A	A	N
9	N	A	A	N
10	Y	B	B	N
11	Y	P	P	N
12	N	A	A	N
13	N	B	B	Y
14	Y	B	B	N
15	N	P	B	N
16	N	A	A	N
17	N	A	A	N
18	N	A	A	N
19	Y	A	A	N
20	N	P	P	N
21	N	B	B	Y
22	N	P	B	N
23	N	B	B	Y
24	N	B	B	Y
25	N	B	P	Y

*ELL = English Language Learners (ESOL/ESL students)

** State Assessment
A= Advanced
P= Proficient;
B= Basic

IEP (Individual Educational Plan) – for students with special needs

d. My Students' Performance Graph

Create and label a graph that shows each student's average performance on Goal/Objective 3. X-axis Label. Set as the X-axis category the student number so that the appropriate student number displays with the appropriate Objective 3 average in the graph. Place it in a new worksheet (tab) on your spreadsheet. Label the graph and the worksheet tab appropriately.

2. Data Analysis and Instructional Decisions

Use your student and class performance averages, graph, and sorted data, as well as the additional student data provided, to complete the narrative reflection statements. As you analyze the data, remember to use precise language and percentages to express the portion of your class that has or has not met the criteria you established in the School Improvement Plan. Write well-developed descriptions and be sure to support your descriptions with student performance data. Use Table 1.5—Using Data to Improve Student Achievement Data Analysis and Instructional Decisions to record your findings and the strategies you suggest.

Data Analysis
a. Examine the students' averages for Objectives 1-3, homework, and attendance. Using percentages, describe how well your class met the three School Improvement Plan goals for student performance, which are:
- Each student will achieve a score of 7 out of 10 on each assessment of each of three targeted objectives from the content curriculum.
- Each student will achieve a score of at least 4 out of 5 for homework completion and accuracy on a scale of 1–5, where a 5 indicates that homework is always complete and accurate.
- Each student will have at least a 95% school attendance rate.

b. Describe patterns you see when you look at attendance and/or homework data and each student's average performance on Goal/Objective 3. Separately describe success on Goal/Objective 3 relative to attendance and homework performance.

c. Describe patterns you see when you look at the "Additional Data" worksheet (ELL, MSA scores, and IEP) and each student's average performance on Goal/Objective 3.

Instructional Decisions
a. Select one of the patterns you described above in Step 2 or 3 related to Goal/Objective 3. Identify and explain specific strategies you would implement to improve student performance based on that pattern. Consider the instructional decisions that teachers make regarding student groupings, learning styles, multiple intelligences, differentiation for special needs, and procedures or policies. While consultation with colleagues or specialists in Special Education or ESOL (English for Speakers of Other Languages) is encouraged, the suggested strategies should be those that the individual teacher can implement on his or her own. It cannot be assumed that any additional staff will be available. In addition, consider only what can be accomplished during regular school hours. No before or after school or lunch time activities should be proposed. Frequently, the students who need the most help are the very students who cannot attend a homework or breakfast club. These students may also be unavailable due to transportation or sibling care situations at home. Consider what can be implemented during class time only.

b. Look at all the performance data, including Table 1.4—Additional Data, and identify other adjustments in instructional strategies that need to be made for the class

Table 1.5. Using Data to Improve Student Achievement Data Analysis and Instructional Decisions

Data Analysis
1. Describe how well your class met the **three school goals** for student performance. • Each student will achieve a score of **7 out of 10 on each assessment** of each of three targeted objectives from the Voluntary State Curriculum. • Each student will achieve a score of at least **4 out of 5 for homework completion and accuracy** on a scale of 1 – 5, where 5 indicates that homework is always complete and accurate. • Each student will have at least a **95% school attendance rate**.
2. Describe patterns you see when you look at attendance and/or homework data and each student's average performance on **Goal/Objective 3**.
3. Describe patterns you see when you look at the "Additional Data" worksheet (ELL, state assessment scores, and IEP) and each student's average performance on **Goal/Objective 3**.
Instructional Decisions
1. Select **one of the patterns** you described above in Step 2 or 3 related to **Goal/Objective 3**. Identify and explain specific strategies you would implement to improve student performance based on that pattern.
2. Look at **all the performance data**, including the "Additional Data" worksheet, and identify other adjustments in instructional strategies that need to be made for the class or group of students. Support your decision based on the data findings.
3. In an actual classroom, you would generally have more information on your students than provided here. With this in mind, describe what additional student information would be useful to make further instructional decisions and explain why that information would be useful.

or group of students. Identify the group that needs assistance and support your decision based on the data findings. Be very specific in proposing instructional strategies to be implemented.

c. In your own classroom, you would generally have more information on your students than provided here. With this in mind, describe what additional student information would be useful to you in making further instructional decisions, and explain why that information would be useful.

This examination of data and its analysis should include following products:
  Completed "(Your Last Name) My Grade Book" workbook with:

- the curriculum standard and three related objectives
- the individual and class averages to one decimal place
- Goal/Objective 3 averages sorted in descending order
- a chart of student average performance on Goal/Objective 3 included as a new object (on the third worksheet tab, labeled appropriately)
- Table 1.5—Using Data to Improve Student Achievement Data Analysis and Instructional Decisions
  addressing items a-c above in "Data Analysis."
  addressing items a-c above in "Instructional Decisions."

Faculty Professional Development

3. Faculty Professional Development Activity on Using Data to Improve Student Achievement

In order to fulfill your role as a leader in the use of data for systemic improvement, you will want to capitalize on your experience with data analysis and the formation of instructional decisions. Identify the components of Activities 1 and 2 with which faculty members need to be familiar in order for them to analyze student data and use it to impact student achievement.

Create an outline of professional development for school faculty on how to:

- create an Excel spreadsheet that includes:
  - three related curriculum objectives from a unit of study or term
  - student assessment scores for those objectives from the target unit of study or term (input from electronic grade book, if available)
  - attendance averages for the unit or term
  - homework completion and accuracy averages for the unit or term
  - individual and class averages for the assessments
  - identification of students with Individual Educational Plans (IEPs)
  - identification of English Language Learners (ELLs)
  - data on state or district-wide assessments for reading and math, if available
- graph the assessment results of at least one of the objectives
- sort the individual averages for at least one of the objectives

Table 1.6. Using Data to Improve Student Achievement Scoring Tool

Criteria	Unacceptable (1)	Acceptable (2)	Competent (3)	Exemplary (4)
My Grade Book Spreadsheet (including individual and class averages)	The three selected objectives are not related, may not support the content area and/or cannot be measured quantitatively	Two of the three selected objectives are related, support the content area and can be measured quantitatively.	The three selected objectives are related, support the content area and can be measured quantitatively	The three selected objectives are related, support the content area and can be measured quantitatively
Required information from state or local school system curriculum planning guide	Minimal required information and data is included, and other information and/or data included may be unclear or irrelevant	Most of the required information and data is included but some unclear and/or irrelevant information or data may be included as well	All required information and data are included.	All required information and data are included.
Student and class averages calculated for each of the three objectives, calculated to one decimal place. Class average calculated for homework and attendance to one decimal place.	Student averages and/or class average are not calculated accurately or may be missing	Only some student averages or resultant class average are calculated accurately.	Most student averages and resultant class average are calculated accurately.	All student averages and class average are calculated accurately.

Criteria	Unacceptable (1)	Acceptable (2)	Competent (3)	Exemplary (4)
My Students' Performance Graph				
Graph illustration of the average performance of each student on Objective 3 on third separate worksheet tab. Correct titles and labels on graph.	Title and all labels are unclear and/or inappropriate or are missing.	Title and most labels are clear and/or appropriate, or some elements are missing.	Title and most of the labels are clear and appropriate; no elements are missing.	Title and all labels are clear and appropriate.
Appropriate selection of type of graph based on the data displayed.	The type of graph selected is clearly inappropriate for the data displayed	The type of graph selected is of questionable appropriateness for the data displayed.	The type of graph selected is appropriate for the data displayed.	The type of graph selected is ideal for the data displayed.
	Graph is incomplete or presented in a format that does not effectively facilitate comparison of student performance and/or may not appear on third worksheet tab	Graph is accurate and presented in a readable format to facilitate comparison of student performance and appears on third worksheet tab	Graph is complete, accurate, and presented in an organized and readable format to facilitate comparison of student performance and appears on third worksheet tab	Graph is complete, accurate, and presented in a well-organized and consistently readable format to effectively facilitate comparison of student performance and appears on appropriately titled third worksheet tab
My Sorted Grade Book				
Sorted averages on Objective 3 in descending order.	Data are not sorted or are sorted inaccurately and/or are displayed in a way that prevents comparisons.	Data are sorted accurately but may be incomplete and/or are displayed in a way that sometimes impedes comparisons.	All required data are sorted accurately and displayed to generally facilitate comparisons.	All required data are sorted accurately and displayed to consistently facilitate comparisons.

(continued)

Table 1.6. (continued)

Criteria	Unacceptable (1)	Acceptable (2)	Competent (3)	Exemplary (4)
Data Analysis Description of how well the class met the three School Improvement Goals	Few or no descriptions are complete or accurate.	Some descriptions are incomplete or may contain inaccuracies.	Most descriptions are generally accurate and complete.	All descriptions are consistently accurate and complete.
Description of a pattern supported by data to identify the relations among attendance, homework, and student performance on Goal/Objective 3 Description of a pattern supported by data to identify the relationship between student performance on Goal/Objective 3 and the "Additional Data"	Patterns are not identified or are identified incorrectly and are not supported by data.	Identified patterns are often inaccurate and/or are inadequately supported by data.	Identified patterns are generally accurate and supported by data.	Identified patterns are consistently accurate and well-supported by data.

Criteria	Unacceptable (1)	Acceptable (2)	Competent (3)	Exemplary (4)
Instructional Decisions				
Identification and explanation of specific strategies to improve student performance based on identified pattern	Strategies are missing or are inappropriate and/or not supported by data	Strategies are sometimes inappropriate or are not clearly identified and/or explanations may not be supported by data	Generally appropriate strategies are identified and explanations are generally logical and supported by data	Consistently appropriate strategies are identified and explanations are consistently logical and well-supported by data
Identification of other needed adjustments in instructional strategies, supported by data findings	Other needed adjustments in instructional strategies are missing or are implausible and/or not supported by data.	Other needed adjustments in instructional strategies are only sometimes plausible and/or are only partially supported by data	Other needed adjustments in instructional strategies are generally plausible and generally supported by data	Other needed adjustments in instructional strategies are consistently plausible and well-supported by data
Identification of useful additional student information and explanation of how it would be used to make instructional decisions.	Explanation of additional student information needed is incomplete and/or is unrealistic or irrelevant to decision-making	Explanation of additional student information needed is incomplete and/or sometimes unrealistic or irrelevant to decision-making	Explanation of additional student information needed is generally realistic and relevant to decision-making	Explanation of additional student information needed is consistently thorough, realistic, and relevant to decision-making

- analyze the data and interpret the findings
- collaborate with grade level or content area colleagues (if possible) to devise instructional strategies to address student needs as described in Activity 2 above

Use Table 1.7 – Using Data Professional Development Outline on which to record the professional development experiences you plan for the faculty in order to acquaint them with the process of data analysis and data-driven decision-making. Consult Table 1.8 – Using Data Professional Development Outline Scoring Tool for further guidelines. Be sure to include the Using Data Professional Development Outline information in Table 2.1 Faculty Technology Professional Growth Plan and Timeline from Chapter 2 Leading with a Shared Vision.

4. Assessment of Additional Faculty Technology Needs

Consider the ongoing technology professional growth needs of a faculty. Often, school district initiatives drive the professional development agenda. However, it is advisable to consult the adult learner regarding professional development needs

Table 1.7. Using Data Professional Development Outline

TOPICS	AUDIENCE	RESOURCES (Equipment and personnel)	TIMEFRAME	PROPOSED TIME OF DAY AND VENUE	RATIONALE FOR SELECTION OF TIME AND VENUE

Table 1.8. Using Data Professional Development Outline Scoring Tool

Criterion	Unacceptable (1)	Acceptable (2)	Competent (3)	Exemplary (4)
TOPICS TO BE COVERED	Few topics essential to a clear understanding of and ability to conduct data analysis and develop instructional strategies are included or are entirely missing.	Some topics essential to a clear understanding of and ability to conduct data analysis and develop instructional strategies are included.	Most topics essential to a clear understanding of and ability to conduct data analysis and develop instructional strategies are included.	All topics essential to a clear understanding of and ability to conduct data analysis and develop instructional strategies are included.
SPECIFIC AUDIENCE	There is little justification for audience selection or there is not audience identified.	A school audience is identified with minimal justification for the selection of that audience.	A school audience is identified with some justification for the selection of that audience.	A specific school audience is identified with an appropriate justification for the selection of that audience.
RESOURCES AND BEST PRACTICES	Software, equipment, and instructional personnel are minimally appropriate or are missing. The needs of the adult learner and/or the complexity of the topics are not reflected in choice of instructional practices.	Some identified software, equipment, and instructional personnel are appropriate. Some of the instructional practices reflect knowledge of the adult learner and are somewhat appropriate for the topics to be covered.	Identified software, equipment, and instructional personnel are mostly appropriate. Most instructional practices reflect knowledge of the adult learner and are appropriate for the topics to be covered.	Essential software, equipment, and appropriate instructional personnel are clearly identified. Instructional practices reflect knowledge of the adult learner and are appropriate for the topics to be covered.
TIMEFRAME	Time allotted to each topic is unrealistic and fails to consider the intended audience and/or topics.	Time allotted to each topic is somewhat realistic and may take the intended audience and/or topics into consideration.	Time allotted to each topic is generally realistic and takes the intended audience and topics into consideration.	Time allotted to each topic is realistic and takes the intended audience and topics into consideration.
PROPOSED TIME OF DAY AND VENUE	The proposed time and/or venue are inappropriate and do not demonstrate an understanding of the needs of the intended audience and the complexity topics to be covered.	The proposed time and venue are somewhat appropriate and superficially demonstrate an understanding of the needs of the intended audience and the complexity topics to be covered.	The proposed time and venue are appropriate and demonstrate an understanding of the needs of the intended audience and the complexity topics to be covered.	The proposed time and venue are appropriate and demonstrate a clear understanding of the needs of the intended audience and the complexity of topics to be covered.
RATIONALE FOR SELECTION OF TIME AND VENUE	A weak rationale is presented for the selection of time and venue that may or may not identify the needs of the intended audience and the configuration of the learning environment.	A rationale is presented for the selection of time and venue that identifies the needs of the intended audience and/or the configuration of the learning environment.	A rationale is presented for the selection of time and venue that identifies the needs of the intended audience and the configuration of the learning environment.	A clear rationale is presented for the selection of time and venue that identifies the needs of the intended audience and the configuration of the learning environment.

as adult learners often learn best when relevance to "self" is established (Knowles, 1970). When there has been a considerable turnover in staff, the need to bring new staff members on board technologically is often immediate. In any event, the efficient and effective use of time and resources dictate that the faculty's technological needs must be prioritized. One way to determine needs is to conduct a survey based on a set of technology standards. Using Table 1.9- Faculty Technology Professional Growth Plan Checklist, survey 6-10 faculty members, asking them to identify 2 areas of immediate need (IN) with regard to their technology skills and one future need in each of the areas of technology use in learning, communication, and productivity (F).

Data Analysis of Faculty Technology Professional Growth Plan Checklist. Assuming that these surveys represent the faculty, analyze and interpret the results to pinpoint the faculty's top two areas of immediate need. In addition, identify one future need in each of the areas of technology use in learning, communication, and productivity. Record that information in Table 1.10 Faculty Technology Professional Growth Plan Checklist Data Analysis. You will want to refer to the information recorded in Table 1.9 when completing the activities in Chapter 4.

Table 1.9. Faculty Technology Professional Growth Plan Checklist

Examine these teacher technology standards to assess your strengths and needs. In the middle column place an (S) next to each Indicator that you would identify as a strength; place an (IN) next to each indicator that you would identify as a personal immediate need; and place an (F) next to each Indicator that you would identify as a future need. Leave the line blank next to any Indicator you feel is neither an area of strength or need.

SEVEN STANDARDS AND OUTCOMES	S IN F	INDICATORS
I. Information Access, Evaluation, Processing and Application Access, evaluate, process and apply information efficiently and effectively.		1. Identify, locate, retrieve and differentiate among a variety of electronic sources of information using technology.
		2. Evaluate information critically and competently for a specific purpose.
		3. Organize, categorize, and store information for efficient retrieval.
		4. Apply information accurately in order to solve a problem or answer a question.
II. Communication A. Use technology effectively and appropriately to interact electronically.		1. Use telecommunications to collaborate with peers, parents, colleagues, administrators and/or experts in the field.
B. Use technology to communicate information in a variety of formats.		1. Select appropriate technologies for a particular communication goal.
		2. Use productivity tools to publish information.
		3. Use multiple digital sources to communicate information online.
III. Legal, Social and Ethical Issues Demonstrate an understanding of the legal, social and ethical issues related to technology use.		1. Identify ethical and legal issues using technology.
		2. Analyze issues related to the uses of technology in educational settings.
		3. Establish classroom policies and procedures that ensure compliance with copyright law, *Fair Use* guidelines, security, privacy and student online protection.
		4. Use classroom procedures to manage an equitable, safe and healthy environment for students.
IV. Assessment for Administration and Instruction Use technology to analyze problems and develop data-driven solutions for instructional and school improvement.		1. Research and analyze data related to student and school performance.
		2. Apply findings and solutions to establish instructional and school improvement goals.
		3. Use appropriate technology to share results and solutions with others, such as parents and the larger community.
V. Integrating Technology into the Curriculum and Instruction Design, implement, and assess learning experiences that incorporate use of technology in a curriculum-related instructional activity to support understanding, inquiry, problem solving, communication and/or collaboration.		1. Assess students' learning/ instructional needs to identify the appropriate technology for instruction.
		2. Evaluate technology materials and media to determine their most appropriate instructional use.
		3. Select and apply research-based practices for integrating technology into instruction.
		4. Use appropriate instructional strategies for integrating technology into instruction.
		5. Select and use appropriate technology to support content-specific student learning outcomes.
		6. Develop an appropriate assessment for measuring student outcomes through the use of technology.
		7. Manage a technology-enhanced environment to maximize student learning.
VI. Assistive Technology Understand human, equity and developmental issues surrounding the use of assistive technology to enhance student learning performance and apply that understanding to practice.		1. Identify and analyze assistive technology resources that accommodate individual student learning needs.
		2. Apply assistive technology to the instructional process and evaluate its impact on learners with diverse backgrounds, characteristics and abilities.
VII. Professional Growth Develop professional practices that support continual learning and professional growth in technology.		1. Create a professional development plan that includes resources to support the use of technology in lifelong learning.
		2. Use resources of professional organizations and groups that support the integration of technology into instruction.
		3. Continually evaluate and reflect on professional practices and emerging technologies to support student learning.
		4. Identify local, state and national standards and use them to improve teaching and learning.

Table 1.10. Faculty Technology Professional Growth Plan Checklist Data Analysis

Current Need #1	
Current Need #2	
Future – Use of Technology in Learning	
Future – Use of Technology in Communication	
Future – Use of Technology in Productivity	

Chapter Two

Leading with a Shared Vision

INTRODUCTION

Successful leaders are often those who anticipate change and proactively pursue a comprehensive plan that incorporates the input and talents of those whom they lead. The principal and her or his administrative colleagues play a vital role in harnessing the power and perspective of their faculty as they analyze data, develop a vision, advocate for change, foster innovation, and develop and monitor implementation of solutions. Working as a team, they make data-driven decisions, identify the need for change, and use research-based practices to give life to the vision. Through collaboration, they create an environment of technology-supported learning that not only enhances instruction, but brings to the students of the 21st century the skills they will need to fully participate in an information-driven world. This vision is a pliable entity that undergoes regular reflection and revision to best meet the instructional needs of the students, the professional development needs of the teaching faculty, and which takes advantage of emerging technologies. All this is done in the full knowledge that advocacy at the state and national level can contribute to bringing the vision to fruition.

The National Technology Standard that promotes visionary leadership is Standard I Educational Administrators inspire and lead development and implementation of a shared vision for comprehensive integration of technology to promote excellence and support transformation throughout the organization.

Educational Administrators

a. inspire and facilitate among all stakeholders a shared vision of purposeful change that maximizes use of digital-age resources to meet and exceed learning goals, support effective instructional practice, and maximize performance of district and school leaders
b. engage in an ongoing process to develop, implement, and communicate technology-infused strategic plans aligned with a shared vision

c. advocate on local, state, and national levels for policies, programs, and funding to support implementation of a technology-infused vision and strategic plan

Activities in the chapter that relate to the design and implementation of a shared vision for technology integration include:

1. Development of a Faculty Technology Professional Growth Plan and Timeline based on analysis of data from the Faculty Technology Professional Growth Plan Checklist (See Chapter 1, Table 1.10)
2. Design of a Professional Growth Plan and Timeline that:
   a. addresses specific immediate needs identified through the administration of the Faculty Technology Professional Growth Plan Checklist (See Chapter 1, Table 1.9)
   b. addresses specific future needs of the faculty in the areas of technology use in learning, communication, and productivity
   c. incorporates the Faculty Professional Development Outline regarding data-driven decision making (See Chapter 1, Table 1.7)
3. Identification of opportunities to advocate for technology, including the identification of appropriate personnel to act as school representatives in an effort to provide leadership experiences for qualified staff

ACTIVITIES

1. Data Analysis of Faculty Professional Growth Needs

Using the assessment of the faculty's technology needs from Chapter 1 and, assuming that the surveys from that chapter represent the faculty at large, analyze and interpret the results of this survey to pinpoint the faculty's top two areas of immediate need. In addition, identify one future need in each of the areas of technology use in learning, communication, and productivity.

2. Faculty Technology Professional Growth Plan and Timeline

Using the Faculty Technology Professional Growth Plan guidelines below, design a year-long professional growth plan to address:
- two of the current areas of immediate need expressed in the surveys
- one need in each of the areas of technology use in learning, communication, and productivity
- the data collection, analysis, and interpretation topic of the Faculty Professional Development Outline (See Chapter 1, Table 1.7)

In your timeline, consider the following:

- resources available to you and your faculty, including print, non-print, electronic, personnel, professional organizations

- the local, state, and/or national standards that support your work
- two areas of current need
- one need to be addressed in the future in the areas of use of technology in learning, in communication, and in productivity
- faculty members with the expertise to assist in the delivery of professional development

Describe each activity you envision, when it will be implemented and/or how often, and what criteria you will use to evaluate the success of each activity.

Faculty Professional Growth Plan

Goal:

Include the following:
- the areas of focus for current professional growth that address two Technology Standard Indicators outlined on the Faculty Technology Professional Growth Plan Checklist that represent the two areas of current need identified
- the areas of focus for future professional growth that address one indicator for each of the following uses of technology:
  - learning
  - communication
  - productivity

Restatement of Goal:

Write a justification for the selected current and future goals that contains a restatement of the goals for the faculty, specifying the technology standards and the indicators from Table 1.9—Faculty Technology Professional Growth Plan Checklist you have identified.

Audience:

Include an explanation of who the faculty will be serving by meeting the identified goals and the ways in which they might do so. For example, this goal could serve one or more of the following: needs of peers or colleagues by contributing to the shared body of knowledge, a group of students with a given need or interest, a school improvement team goal, a district mandate, a federal mandate.

A. Conducting Research on Resources

What activities, contacts and resources are necessary to reach your goal?
Resources (list books and/or websites):
What professional organizations will you recommend as faculty resources?
What emerging technology(ies) will you highlight that support the areas of focus you have identified?
What local, state and/or national standards will you cite in your professional development presentations?

B. Devising a Plan of Action

> Through what behaviors, products, or performances might the faculty demonstrate that they are approaching or meeting each of the identified goals?
> Current Need #1:
> Current Need #2:
> Current Need #3:
> Future Use of Technology in Learning:
> Future Use of Technology in Communication:
> Future Use of Technology in Productivity:

3. Advocating Technology

Identify potential opportunities to advocate for technology, including, but not limited to, budget hearing boards, county boards of education, grant opportunities, PTA councils, etc. Include information on personnel for whom you would like to provide leadership experience who might represent your school at these advocacy opportunities. Record the information using Table 2.2 Potential Opportunities for Technology Advocacy.

Table 2.1. Faculty Technology Professional Growth Plan Timeline

Create a timeline, goal and description of activities to be included in the implementation of the professional growth plan, and a description of how you will know, by performances or behaviors, that faculty members have made progress or have met the goal of the activities.

GOAL AND DESCRIPTION OF ACTIVITY	WHEN? HOW OFTEN?	QUALIFIED SCHOOL STAFF WHO MAY ASSIST	CRITERIA FOR EVALUATION
Current Need #1			
Activity #1			
Activity #2			
Current Need #2			
Activity #1			
Activity #2			

(*continued*)

Table 2.1. Faculty Technology Professional Growth Plan Timeline

GOAL AND DESCRIPTION OF ACTIVITY	WHEN? HOW OFTEN?	QUALIFIED SCHOOL STAFF WHO MAY ASSIST	CRITERIA FOR EVALUATION
Using Data to Improve Student Achievement			
Professional Development Outline from Chapter 1, Table 2.1			
Future – Use of Technology in Learning			
Activity			
Future – Use of Technology in Communication			
Activity			
Future – Use of Technology in Productivity			
Activity			

Table 2.2. Potential Opportunities for Advocacy

What opportunities for technology advocacy exist in your school and/or school system? Are there budget hearings in which faculty members may participate? What grant opportunities might be investigated? Are there strategic partnerships that may be beneficial for the school and community alike? Administrators are in a unique position in that they can encourage and foster leadership within their own school by recognizing the talents of faculty members Administrators can "grow" leaders by extending opportunities for technology advocacy to faculty members who exhibit a talent and interest in such activities. Outline below potential forums for technology advocacy within your school system. Identify key personnel and their position.

ADVOCACY TOPIC	AUDIENCE OR VENUE	SCHOOL REPRESENTATIVE	POSITION OR LEVEL OF EXPERIENCE OF REPRESENTATIVE*

Table 2.3. Faculty Technology Professional Growth Plan Technology and Timeline Advocacy Potential Scoring Tool

Criterion	Unacceptable (1)	Acceptable (2)	Competent (3)	Exemplary (4)
Justification	The Technology Standard and the Indicator(s) representing the two areas of current faculty need and the three areas of future need addressed in goal may be incomplete or are missing	The Technology Standard and the Indicator(s) representing the two areas of current faculty need and the three areas of future need addressed in goal may not be clearly specified.	The Technology Standard and the Indicator(s) representing the two areas of current faculty need and the three areas of future need addressed in goal are specified.	The Technology Standard and the Indicator(s) representing the two areas of current faculty need and the three areas of future need addressed in goal are clearly specified.
	Explains who will be served by meeting the goal.	Minimally explains who will be served by meeting the goal.	Somewhat explains who will be served by meeting the goal.	Clearly explains who will be served by meeting the goal.
Resources	Cites few books, websites, professional organizations, emerging technologies, and national, state, or local standards that support the professional growth timeline activities or citation of resources may be inappropriate or missing.	Cites some books, websites, professional organizations, emerging technologies, and national, state, or local standards that support the professional growth timeline activities.	Cites books, websites, professional organizations, emerging technologies, and national, state, or local standards that support the professional growth timeline activities.	Cites a wide range of useful books, websites, professional organizations, emerging technologies, and national, state, or local standards that clearly support the professional growth timeline activities.
Faculty Products or Performances	Faculty products or performances are inappropriate or missing.	Vague faculty products or performances for each of the two current and the three future needs are identified.	Faculty products or performances are identified for each of the two current and the three future needs.	Specific and appropriate faculty products or performances are clearly identified for each of the two current and the three future needs.

Criterion	Unacceptable (1)	Acceptable (2)	Competent (3)	Exemplary (4)
Professional Growth Activities, Frequency, and Evaluation	Activities are identified that may or may not respond to the faculty needs	A few appropriate activities that respond to some of the faculty needs	Mostly appropriate activities that respond to some of the faculty needs	Specific appropriate activities that respond to each of the faculty needs
	Frequency is missing	Frequency is stated, but may be inappropriate	Frequency is somewhat inappropriate	Appropriate frequency guidelines
	Qualified faculty with the expertise to assist are missing	A few qualified faculty with the expertise to assist are identified	Some qualified faculty with the expertise to assist	Appropriate, qualified faculty with the expertise to assist
	Evaluation criteria are inappropriate or may be missing	Few appropriate evaluation criteria are specified	Mostly appropriate evaluation criteria are specified	Specific, appropriate evaluation criteria are identified
	The Using Data to Improve Student Achievement professional growth Activity from Chapter 1 is missing	A few aspects of the Using Data to Improve Student Achievement professional growth Activity from Chapter 1 are included	Many aspects of the Using Data to Improve Student Achievement professional growth Activity from Chapter 1 are included	All appropriate aspects of the Using Data to Improve Student Achievement professional growth Activity from Chapter 1 are included
Potential for Advocacy	Audiences, venues, topics, or personnel are either inappropriate or are not identified	Few audiences or venues, topics, or appropriate personnel are identified	Some potential audiences or venues, topics, and appropriate personnel are clearly identified	A wide range of potential audiences or venues, topics, and appropriate personnel are clearly identified

Chapter Three

Navigating the Digital Culture: Social, Legal and Ethical Issues

INTRODUCTION

As an administrator, you are required to act with justice and integrity. Your ethical philosophy is the motivating factor in your daily actions. Our complex society challenges us to review our thoughts and daily habits. The following chapter and assignments are designed to assist you in a reflective process regarding technology issues and the use of digital information, as well as issues of equal access, privacy, health, safety and the law. This knowledge will be used to isolate and define the technology use or misuse in your school or at the district level.

The National Technology Standard that charges administrators to be models and facilitators of technological ethical behavior is Standard V. Educational Administrators:

a. ensure equitable access to appropriate digital tools and resources to meet the needs of all learners
b. promote, model, and establish policies for safe, legal, and ethical use of digital information and technology
c. promote and model responsible social interactions related to the use of technology and information
d. model and facilitate the development of a shared cultural understanding and involvement in global issues through the use of contemporary communication and collaboration tools

Activities in this chapter that relate to issues of digital citizenship include:

1. Completion of the Reflection on Present Knowledge
2. Completion of the Internet Search for sites that identify the legal, ethical, privacy, health, safety, and equal access issues related to the use of technology in the educational setting
3. Completion of the Social, Legal and Ethical Issues Search Log
4. An informal review of brief case scenarios
5. A final document that includes:

A. A review of a case study in which you identify the social, legal, ethical, health, safety, security, and privacy issues related to the case study. A case study report is required along with observations and equal access information.
B. Two observations of faculty members conducted in departments/grade levels in your building (or district). If classroom observations are not possible, then encounters with these issues from personal experience, media references, and other sources of information may be described.

   Identify and describe instances of either the proper or improper use of technology regarding:
   - legal or ethical issues you have observed, one being a copyright issue with specific reference to the law/s
   - security and privacy issues observed
   - health and safety issues, citing the policies implemented properly or in violation
C. Identification of technology resources in your building. What is/are the current need/s to ensure equal access for all learners and educators (Refer to Chapter 2, Assignment 1, from Standard I)?

ACTIVITIES

1. Reflection on Present Knowledge

Record your reflections on the following questions:

a. What do you presently know about:
   - student and faculty acceptable use policies and copyright law as they pertain to education
   - health and safety issues associated with the classroom and technology use
   - privacy issues related to student information and work
b. What is the Children's Internet Protection Act?
   www.fcc.gov/cgb/consumerfacts/cipa.html
c. What new laws and regulations will effect school or district policy?
d. What present policy does your school or district have in regards to technology?
e. What is the vehicle for informing the faculty about these issues?
f. Do parents and/or students sign a technology contract or acceptable use policy?
   What are the essential issues covered within this contract?
g. As an administrator either at the local or district level, what possible steps might you implement to improve faculty and student knowledge of ethical and legal issues regarding technology?

2. Internet Search

Conduct an Internet search to identify the technological legal, ethical, privacy, security, health, safety, and equal access issues associated with technology use in the educational setting. This search serves as part of the research informing the PowerPoint presentation for Chapter 4: Technology and Its Impact on Professional Practice.

The following sites might be helpful to your search.

http://www.findlaw.com
http://www.oyez.org/
http://fairuse.stanford.edu/
http://www.supremecourtus.gov

3. Social, Legal Ethical Search Log

While searching for useful sites on this topic, use the search log template below to keep a record of your findings. Evaluate the sites you have located in light of the website evaluative criteria found at http://www.library.cornell.edu/olinuris/ref/webcrit.html.

a. Keep a record of your searches as well as 3–4 keywords and 1 query (combination of keywords) that effectively guided the search
b. Identify at least 4 websites. Include a wide variety of appropriate electronic resources
c. Consistently evaluate the websites using appropriate evaluative criteria from the site above

Social Legal Ethical Issues Search Log
  What query (keywords) did you use to guide your search?
    Website #1
      Search Engine used:
      Name and URL
      Website Evaluation Notes (Use evaluative criteria from http://www.library.cornell.edu/olinuris/ref/webcrit.html
    Website #2
      Search Engine used:
      Name and URL
      Website Evaluation Notes (Use evaluative criteria from http://www.library.cornell.edu/olinuris/ref/webcrit.html
    Website #3
      Search Engine used:
      Name and URL
      Website Evaluation Notes (Use evaluative criteria from http://www.library.cornell.edu/olinuris/ref/webcrit.html
    Website #4
      Search Engine used:
      Name and URL
      Website Evaluation Notes (Use evaluative criteria from http://www.library.cornell.edu/olinuris/ref/webcrit.html

Table 3.1. Search Log Scoring Tool

Criterion	Unacceptable (1)	Acceptable (2)	Competent (3)	Exemplary (4)
Skill in researching information using keywords in an effective query	Log includes insufficient key words or an ineffective query to guide the search for information.	Log includes at least 1-2 key words and 1 query that somewhat effectively guide the search for information.	Log includes 3-4 key words and 1 query that generally guide the search for information.	Log includes 3-4 key words and 1 query that effectively guide the search for information.
	The website name or URL are missing.	Both website name and URL are provided.	Both website name and URL are provided.	Both website name and URL are provided.
Range of electronic resources	Log identifies fewer than 4 sites from a very narrow range of electronic resources, some of which may be inappropriate.	Log fewer than 4 sites and/or identifies a limited range of appropriate electronic resources.	Log identifies at least 4 sites from a variety of appropriate electronic resources.	Log identifies at least 4 sites from a wide variety of appropriate electronic resources
Evaluation of resources using appropriate criteria	Sources were not consistently evaluated and/or did not use appropriate evaluation criteria.	Sources were minimally evaluated using appropriate evaluation criteria.	Sources were generally evaluated using appropriate evaluation criteria.	Sources were consistently evaluated using appropriate evaluation criteria.

Developed from Maryland's *Preparing Tomorrow's Teachers to Use Technology (PT3)*, USDOE Catalyst Grant P342A990201, May 2002.

4. Informal Scenario Review

Review the following scenarios. Identify the technological legal (including copyright and equal access), ethical, privacy, security, health, safety, and concerns. Cite laws and policy. Describe what actions you might take as an administrator.

Case Study Scenarios

A. Beverly, a high school student, has invited Jake, her friend, to listen to a new CD that she has purchased. Jake is the usual disc jockey for school dances. Beverly suggested that this particular CD would be great for the dance this Friday. Jake regularly copies music CDs and arranges the copied music in his own way for the upcoming dances. You are attending the dance as a chaperone. Beverly is one of the student representatives and has established a friendly rapport with you. She is excited about the music for tonight and she explains her influence in the selection for the dance.

   What steps might you take as an administrator?

B. Mr. Davis regularly uses his email for personal messages. In an email to a friend, he noted that, since the school's technology funds were limited, he decided to load software with a single user license on each of the lab computers. He emails his friend that the lessons in the lab are going much more effectively now that the students have meaningful activities to do on the computer. Another teacher, who is acquainted with Mr. Davis' email friend, mentions this to you during a discussion in your office about the computer lab schedule.

   What might you do?

C. The English teacher has assigned a term-paper for her class. One of the students, Judy, has identified a topic for her English term-paper. Since Judy works every evening, she finds that she has limited time to develop her paper herself. One evening, she found that someone else has posted a paper on her topic online. She paid for a copy of the paper and handed it in for her assignment. The teacher is very impressed and praises Judy for such fine work. The teacher intends to select this student for an award at the end of the year. Judy is the daughter of one of the teacher's best friends. Later in the week, another student from Judy's class comes to you and explains what she knows about where Judy's paper came from.

   What might you do?

D. Mr. Jacobs, the science teacher, has found a cool website. For an affordable price, he can download movies and save them. The movie he downloaded will fit nicely into his science class. The special effects in the movie actually demonstrate interesting physics concepts. You overhear Mr. Jacobs as he tells another physics teacher about

his amazing find and offers to lend the video to that teacher after he uses the video during his lesson the following day.
What might you do?

E. As one of the resources for group projects, the health teacher has posted several articles about environmental dangers of nuclear power plants and weapons. Your son, Lee, is in his class. Lee is particularly interested in an article that describes "jelly babies" in the South Pacific Islands for his group project. He downloads this article and makes several copies for himself and a few friends. He is very interested in sharing this article with you, as well, and gives you a copy.
What might you do?

F. Ms. Britain is an exceptional teacher. She prepares her work diligently. She is not too familiar with the computer software that she hopes to use in an effort to incorporate technology in one of her lessons. She wants to work in the lab after school. The technology teacher is the only one with a key to the computer lab. He generally leaves promptly at 3:30 pm. Ms. Britain's last class doesn't end until 3:30 pm. Ms. Britain wants to stay after school to learn the software that she intends to use with her class. The technology teacher tells her that she can not use the lab after 3:30 pm. Ms. Britain approaches you with her problem.
What might you do as an administrator?

G. Your district's technology plan calls for the replacement of non-functioning or out-of-date computers. In this year's budget, spending on technology was severely curtailed. The husband of the assistant superintendent in your district owns a small computer business. He offers the district a large discount to purchase with his company.
What might you do?

5. Case Study and Observations: Technology Issues in the Educational Setting

A. Case Study Analysis

Read the case study below. Answer the questions regarding violations below:

Case Study:
You are a student teacher at Greater Maryland Middle School. Today you are observing Mrs. Jones teaching her social studies class in the computer lab. Her first period is her planning period. She has asked you to assist her with setting up the lab for her lesson plan. She is installing the school's only copy of an atlas software program for a single user license on the 22 computers in the lab. She explains that her lesson will require students to download information about the country that they have been assigned from the atlas program and to also search the Internet for more information

for a PowerPoint presentation. Mrs. Jones encourages students to freely use any information from the Internet for their presentation.

At the beginning of each class, the students enter and sit where they choose, occasionally arguing over seats. For the four classes with more than 22 students, Mrs. Jones pairs a boy and a girl, assigning the boy to operate the computer and the girl to take notes. Mrs. Jones starts the class by sharing a model of a final product, a PowerPoint presentation. Without guidance, she encourages the students to freely copy any graphics and text from the Internet to brighten up their slides. She explains that they will have one day in the computer lab to complete the assignment and that, if they do not finish in class, they must complete the work at home within two days. She directs them to use the atlas software and to search the web for sites about the country assigned to them. At the completion of class, she gives them time to save their work to the class folder on the local area network and reminds them not to access other folders. During the first class period with students, a few students become distracted with the computer in the first row where Mrs. Jones had been working on her grade book program at the end of her planning period. They begin reciting aloud the classmates' scores that are still visible on the monitor. She closes the program and puts the students back on task. Several students sitting by the windows complain that they cannot read their monitors due to glare.

During the next class, Period 3, several students rush in and sit toward the back of the lab while the teacher does hall duty. As the other students enter the class, they become interested in the stifled giggles from the back row. The bell rings and the teacher enters the room approaching the group of students huddled in the back around a monitor. She disperses the group and finds the monitor displaying a commercial web site for movie videos. She proceeds as she did with the previous class. When the bell rings at the end of class, several students rush out without properly logging out and the backpack of one gets hooked to a monitor cable. Luckily, a student nearby catches the monitor before it falls.

Period 4 begins more smoothly than the last, except for a brief delay to locate a workstation for a wheelchair-bound student. One student has already started the assignment at home and has brought his work on disk. He opens the file and continues his work.

Several minutes into the 5th period, the guidance counselor brings a student new to the school and introduces her to Mrs. Jones. The counselor explains that her mother is downstairs completing the entrance paperwork. Mrs. Jones briefly describes the assignment and seats the new girl next to another student accessing the Internet.

The day concludes with a smooth opening to period 6; however, 15 minutes into the class, the power to the lab server goes out. Mrs. Jones calms the excited students and asks them to be patient, assuming the power will be on within a few minutes. The principal makes an announcement that a local power surge affected the server and the lab computers will be down for the remainder of the day. Since there are 35 minutes left until dismissal, he encourages teachers to continue their lessons. Mrs. Jones mentions to you that she really had nothing else planned and she does not want to begin the next day's lesson, which would put the classes out of sync with each other. She tells the students they will have to complete the project on their own and allows them to talk quietly until the dismissal bell rings. After the final bell, Mrs. Jones dismisses the students and tells you to reflect on the day.

Developed from Maryland's *Preparing Tomorrow's Teachers to Use Technology (PT3),* USDOE Catalyst Grant P342A990201, May 2002

Using the case study, answer the following questions:

1. Underline or highlight all questionable practices that you noted in the case study.
2. Of those legal and ethical issues (one of which must deal with copyright), identify three different issues that arise from this case study and explain what laws, policies and/or procedures are most applicable to each issue.
3. Of those health and safety considerations raised in the case study, identify three. Suggest one potential way of addressing each of the issues you identified, including classroom management techniques that may facilitate a safe and orderly environment.
4. Of those security and/or privacy issues raised in the case study, pick three. For each instance, describe the policies and procedures that may help ensure security and privacy.
5. The case study highlights advantages and disadvantages of widespread use of, and reliance upon, technology in the classroom.

Identify one advantage and describe how it impacts technology use in educational settings. Support your answer with examples based upon your prior knowledge and experience.

Identify one disadvantage and describe how it impacts technology use in educational settings. Support your answer with examples based upon your prior knowledge and experience.

Developed from Maryland's *Preparing Tomorrow's Teachers to Use Technology (PT3),* USDOE Catalyst Grant P342A990201, May 2002.

B. Classroom Observation (or Media and Experiential Knowledge)

Administrators are required to monitor the proper use of technology as a tool for learning. One means of assessing the degree to which legal, social, and ethical uses of technology are implemented in the school setting is to conduct classroom observations. Use the following observation form for two classroom observations. Write a final analysis of combined classroom observations that addresses the proper or improper use of technology in the areas of law, ethics, health and safety and equal access. As an administrator discuss how you will respond to what you have observed to be the status of use of technology. If actual classroom observations are not possible, use the guide questions below to record your own experiences with these issues and/or examples currently found in the media.

The observed lesson notes or reflection on personal experiences and media include:

1. comments on technology use with regard to legal and ethical guidelines, including copyright and equal access guidelines
2. comments on the learning environment with regard to health and safety guidelines, including classroom management and space configuration
3. comments on technology use with regard to classroom security and privacy guidelines
4. comments on adherence to equal access policies

The summary of classroom observation or experiences and current information from the media on the topic includes:

C. Identification of Resources for the Purposes of Assuring Equal Access

Conversation surrounding the "digital divide" highlights the need for administrators to be sensitive to the issue of equal access. Just as lesson design should reflect this approach, an administrator's approach to facilities for students and staff must be guided by the principle of equal access. In what way can an administrator identify facilities needs in order to ensure equal access to all learners and educators? (Refer to Chapter 1 Interviews).

- Describe school or district demographics. Describe socioeconomic composition of student body.
- Summarize technology that is available to teachers and students (# of computers per faculty member; student-to-computer ratio)
- As a prospective administrator, what are the greatest needs of your school to ensure equal access to all learners and educators?
- As a prospective administrator, how might you address these needs?

Table 3.2. Case Study and Observation/Reflection Scoring Tool

The first four criteria listed in the case study can be scored using the first six criteria
The required classroom observations can be scored using the last three sets of criteria.

Criteria	Unacceptable (1)	Acceptable (2)	Competent (3)	Exemplary (4)
Responses to case study identified the nature of three examples of legal and ethical technology use, including issues of equal access and at least one dealing with copyright	One or fewer legal or ethical issues were addressed or issues were minimally addressed without support of laws and policies.	Two to three legal and ethical issues, including at least one dealing with copyright, were addressed and were explained, but without support of the laws and policies.	Three legal and ethical issues, including at least one dealing with copyright, were sufficiently addressed and were clearly explained with support of the laws and policies.	Three legal and ethical issues, including at least one dealing with copyright, were thoroughly addressed and were logically explained with support of the laws and policies.
Interventions or strategies to be implemented by the teacher were identified for each issue cited.	Strategies and/or interventions were inappropriate and/or no strategies or interventions were identified.	At least two appropriate strategies or interventions were identified.	Strategies and/or interventions were identified for each of the three issues cited.	Well-developed strategies and/or interventions were identified for each of the three issues cited.
Responses to case study identified the nature of three examples of health and safety issues associated with the use of technology.	One or fewer health and safety issues were addressed or issues were minimally addressed.	Two to three health and safety issues were addressed.	Three health and safety issues were addressed and were supported with current literature.	Three health and safety issues were thoroughly addressed and were supported with knowledge of current issues addressed in academic literature.
Interventions or strategies to be implemented by the teacher were identified for each issue cited.	Strategies and/or interventions were inappropriate and/or no strategies or interventions were identified.	At least two appropriate strategies and/or interventions were identified.	Strategies and/or interventions were identified for each of the three issues cited.	Well-developed strategies and/or interventions were identified for each of the three issues cited.

(continued)

Table 3.2. Case Study and Observation/Reflection Scoring Tool

Criteria	Unacceptable (1)	Acceptable (2)	Competent (3)	Exemplary (4)
Responses to case study identified the nature of three examples of security and privacy issues associated with the use of technology	One or fewer security and privacy issues were identified or issues were minimally addressed.	Two to three security and privacy issues were identified but policies were not clearly explained.	Three security and privacy issues were identified and policies were adequately explained.	Three privacy and security issues were clearly identified and policies were thoroughly explained.
Interventions or strategies to be implemented by the teacher were identified for each issue cited	Strategies and/or interventions were inappropriate and/or no strategies or interventions were identified.	At least two appropriate strategies and/or interventions were identified.	Strategies and/or interventions were identified for each of the three issues cited.	Well-developed strategies and/or interventions were identified for each of the three issues cited.
Classroom Observations/Reflection Regarding Legal and Ethical Issues, Including Copyright and Equal Access	Observations/reflections were vague in identifying legal and ethical issues or none were identified.	Observations/reflections noted proper and/or improper legal and/or ethical use of technology.	Observations/reflection noted proper and/or improper legal and/or ethical use of technology.	The four required observations examined the proper or improper legal and/or ethical use of technology.
		Present laws or policy may not have been used for support.	An attempt to support observations with present laws and policies was made.	Legal and ethical issues were analyzed and supported with laws and policies.
			Proposed changes may have been included.	Observation reflections listed possible ways to improve setting.

Navigating the Digital Culture: Social, Legal and Ethical Issues 45

Criteria	Unacceptable (1)	Acceptable (2)	Competent (3)	Exemplary (4)
Classroom Observations/Reflection Regarding Health and Safety Issues	Observations/reflections were vague in identifying health and safety issues or none were identified.	Observations/reflection noted a presence and/or lack of attention to health and safety issues. Present laws or policy may not have been used for support.	General health and safety issues were clearly identified. Proposed changes may have been included.	General and specific health and safety issues were clearly identified. Observation/reflection reflections listed possible ways to improve setting.
Classroom Observations/Reflection Regarding Privacy and Security Issues	Observations/reflections were vague in identifying privacy and security issues or none were identified.	Observations/reflection noted a presence and/or lack of attention to privacy and security issues. Present laws or policy may not have been used for support.	General privacy and security issues were clearly identified. Proposed changes may have been included.	General and specific privacy and security issues were clearly identified. Observation/reflections reflections listed possible ways to improve setting.

Chapter Four

Technology and Its Impact on Professional Practice

INTRODUCTION

While the advent of technology may not have given administrators more time to relax, it certainly has provided varied tools and resources with which educators can be more efficient and productive. Perhaps never before have administrators been in such a position to promote empowerment and innovation. This chapter focuses on activities for your reflection and practice to increase and enhance your productivity, as well as that of your faculty and staff; to promote collaboration within a strong learning community; and to foster technology integration and innovation.

The National Technology Standard that promotes an environment of professional learning and innovation through the integration of contemporary technologies is Standard III. Educational Administrators:

a. allocate time, resources, and access to ensure ongoing professional growth in technology fluency and integration
b. facilitate and participate in learning communities that stimulate, nurture, and support administrators, faculty, and staff in the study and use of technology
c. promote and model effective communication and collaboration among stakeholders using digital-age tools
d. stay abreast of educational research and emerging trends regarding effective use of technology and encourage evaluation of new technologies for their potential to improve student learning

Modeling effective communication and collaboration are part of the responsibilities of an administrator. To that end, the final result of the work from this chapter will be a PowerPoint presentation to a target audience, such as faculty and staff, students, or parents. The creation of the presentation is dependent on your successful completion of Social, Legal and Ethical activities from Chapter 3 and the insights you have already gathered on the needs of your school. The presentation may be designed as the centerpiece of a professional growth experience for the faculty and staff. It should be based on information gathered on access to and the implementation of the existing technology tools and should highlight the legal, ethical, and safe use of those technologies and digital resources. The activities involving research from Chapter 3 should assist you in focusing on the elements of school law associated with technology use and integration. The PowerPoint presentation should share with your target audience instances of improper uses of technology and should inform them of ways to proactively address the legal, ethical, and safety considerations as found in your research on Social, Legal and Ethical and Ethical concerns (Chapter 3, Standard V).

Activities in this chapter include:
1. Summary of technology resources and skill needs
2. A personal assessment of present use of technology and needs
3. Faculty interviews to assess the present use by and needs of faculty members
4. A summary of the data from faculty surveys
5. Student interviews for present and future use of technology
6. A summary of the data from student input

   Completion of the activities from Chapter 3: Navigating the Digital Culture is a prerequisite to the following activities:
7. Summary of data collected from Social, Legal, Ethical concerns
8. Creation of a PowerPoint presentation based on the summary information collected from activities 4, 6, and 7. Prepare this PowerPoint presentation for a specific audience or audiences such as, faculty, staff, students, parents or other related groups. It may form all or part of a professional development activity for your faculty.

ACTIVITIES

1. Technology Resources Summary

You have already reviewed the technology resources in your building in Chapter 1. Additionally, you have surveyed the faculty to determine their current and future technology skill needs in Chapter 2. To isolate the top three priorities to be addressed, complete the Technology Resources questions below (Refer to activities from Chapter 1 and 2, if necessary).

Technology Integration and Use of Digital Resources

1. What is your school/district doing well in the field of technology?
    a.
    b.
    c.

2. What were recognized as the current needs of your school or district?
    a.
    b.
    c.

2. Personal Assessment

What is your personal perspective on the use of technologies and digital resources in your school? Complete the questions below:

a. Identify the various technology hardware that you use regularly.
b. Identify hardware that you would like to use if you knew how.
c. Identify the software that you regularly use.
d. In what ways does the software that you use enhance your productivity or ability to produce, collaborate on, and share information?
e. What emerging technologies and/or innovative software are you aware of that you like to investigate further?
f. How might those technologies and/or software improve your effectiveness?
g. What does the school or district use to gather and organize the following data:

   grading
   discipline records
   absenteeism
   scheduling
   communication
   publishing (hard copy publications or online)
   searching
   budget
   testing and assessment

h. What are your professional development needs with regard to technology use and/or innovation?

3. Faculty Interviews

How does the faculty view the allocation of technology tools and the appropriateness of professional development in order for faculty to effectively integrate them? Using the questions a through h above, survey up to four faculty members.

4. Summarize the Data from the Faculty Surveys

a. What technology equipment is use regularly?
b. What do you, as a teacher and/or prospective administrator, and the current faculty see as valuable additions to present technological equipment?
c. List the software that is in regular use.
d. How does this software enhance school-wide productivity or ability to produce, collaborate on, and share information?
e. What emerging technologies and/or innovative software was identified most frequently as having potential application for teachers and/or administrators?
f. How might these emerging technologies and/or this software assist the productivity of the faculty? Explain.

g. After gathering data on the technology tools and software that the school or district uses to compile and organize important information, how would you evaluate the current allocation of and access to these resources within the school/district? *Circle the grade.*

Grading	A	B	C	D	F
Discipline Records	A	B	C	D	F
Absenteeism	A	B	C	D	F
Scheduling	A	B	C	D	F
Communication	A	B	C	D	F
Publishing	A	B	C	D	F
Searching	A	B	C	D	F
Budget	A	B	C	D	F
Testing/Assessment	A	B	C	D	F

h. For 5 of the 9 grades above that are less than an A, suggest how you might make improvements.
i. Do faculty members have equal access?
j. Considering the financial needs of your school and the importance of equal access, what changes would you actually make in new hardware/software that would benefit the faculty?

5. Student Interviews

Interview several students. Ask them to describe the technologies and software they would suggest for their ideal computer lab.

a. What is your favorite technology to use?
b. Do you use this technology for academic purposes?
c. What technologies are available for your use in school? Which of these do you use?
d. What emerging or additional technology would you like the school to have to assist you in your academic pursuits?
e. Draw the layout for the ideal academic technology lab. Label equipment.
f. Who should be able to use this lab?

6. Student Input

Summarize the data from the student surveys.

a. What is the favorite student technology that was cited?
b. To what extent is it used in academic?
c. What emerging or additional technologies did the students cite as valuable in academics?
d. Do you see these requests as a possibility, given your school's/district's current technology funding? Explain.

e. What unique information did the student input provide?
f. What changes would you make for students?

7. Social, Legal Ethical Summary

As a planning tool for your PowerPoint presentation, summarize the data from your research on Legal, Social, and Ethical concerns from the activities completed in Chapter 3, for Standard V.

a. What does the target audience (faculty, staff, students or parents) need to know about new laws and regulations?
b. What changes need to be made in the faculty Acceptable Use Policy and/or in the student version regarding software and the use of the Internet?
c. How have faculty and students been using technology ethically and legally?
d. Is there ethical or legal information that the target audience needs to know?
e. From your observations, experiences, scenarios, and media coverage, summarize improper uses of technology and the ethical issues related to that use.
f. Prioritize and decide the specific information you will address in the PowerPoint presentation.
g. Identify areas of continued concern in regard to:
   Acceptable use policy
   Copyright
   Health and safety
   Privacy and security
   Children's Internet Protection Act
h. What should be included in your PowerPoint from section g?

8. PowerPoint Presentation

Create a PowerPoint presentation based on the information collected from activities 4, 6, and 7. This PowerPoint is designed to be an informative presentation for a target audience, such as, faculty, staff, students, parents or other school group, and should also include references to research sources. In deciding on your target audience, ask yourself:

- Will this presentation be for the school board to inform them of teacher/student needs, as well as legal and ethical considerations?
- Is it designed to inform faculty and/or staff about appropriate legal, ethical, health and safety, and security and privacy practices?
- Are students the target audience for the PowerPoint presentation as a means to identify improper uses and suggest alternatives for the use of technology?

As an administrator, it is important to model and inform school faculty and staff, and other stakeholders about the wide variety of issues associated with the use of technology. In this way, not only are staff members informed, but they are prepared to share guidelines for legal, ethical, and safe computer use with students. If the target audience is the faculty and/or staff, keep in mind the collaborative learning environment you want to create surrounding the professional development of which the PowerPoint is a vital part. Consider what faculty and staff may already know about the topics to be presented and be sure to activate that prior knowledge so that the target audience has something on which to build. Incorporate opportunities for interaction with and among the audience members.

The PowerPoint should include:

- Current needs in order to ensure equal access
- Elements that describe current best practices in social, legal, privacy, security and ethical concerns
- Elements that describe current best practices regarding health and safety
- A variety of recent references from a college library database, including at least one primary source to support the presentation
- Complete presentation notes for the instructor (which can be included in the Notes area of Normal View in PowerPoint)
- handout/s of useful sites for your intended audience
-

CHAPTER END REFLECTION QUESTIONS

How can the use of technology make administrators more efficient and effective?
How are administrators more productive as a result of the use of technology?
In what ways can an administrator facilitate faculty participation in the study and use of technology?
In what ways can an administrator improve the faculty's satisfaction with their use of technology?

Table 4.1. Social, Legal, and Ethical Uses of Technology PowerPoint Presentation Scoring Tool

Criterion	Unacceptable (1)	Acceptable (2)	Competent (3)	Exemplary (4)
Identification of present school resources, teacher and student needs	Issues were not addressed	Needs of the school were identified. Teacher and student issues were addressed.	Some needs of the school were identified. Teacher and student issues were addressed adequately.	Clear needs of the school were identified. Teacher and student issues were addressed thoroughly.
Identification of examples of technological legal and ethical issues and/or their misuse	Legal and ethical issues were not addressed	Legal and ethical issues were addressed and were explained but without support from the laws and policies	Legal and ethical issues were sufficiently addressed and were clearly explained with support from the laws and policies	Legal and ethical issues were thoroughly addressed and were logically explained with support from the laws and policies
Identification of examples of technological health and safety issues	Health and safety issues were not addressed or minimally addressed.	Health and safety issues were addressed but were not supported with literature.	Health and safety issues were addressed and were supported with current literature.	Health and safety issues were thoroughly addressed and were supported with ample knowledge of current issues addressed in academic literature.
Identification of security and privacy issues	Privacy issues were not identified nor were present policies in this regard.	Privacy issues were identified but policies were not clearly explained.	Privacy issues were identified and policies were adequately explained.	Privacy issues were clearly identified and policies were thoroughly explained.
Identification of equal access issues	Equal access issues were not identified.	Equal access issues were minimally identified.	Equal access issues were clearly identified but without a clear educational rationale.	Equal access issues were clearly identified with educational rationale.

Criterion	Unacceptable (1)	Acceptable (2)	Competent (3)	Exemplary (4)
PowerPoint Presentation - Best Practices	Selections of font size, color, slide background color or design made the presentation illegible.	Selections of font size, color, slide background color or design were somewhat effective.	Selections of font size, color, slide background color or design were mostly effective. Candidate was creative in his/her presentation.	Selections of font size, color, slide background color or design were consistently effective and enhanced the presentation.
	Graphics, animations, slide transitions, or sound effects may have detracted from the presentation.	Aspects of the presentation, such as graphics, animations, slide transitions, or sound effects may have detracted from the presentation.	Most elements of the presentation, including graphics, animations, slide transitions, or sound effects enhanced the presentation.	Graphics, animations, slide transition, and/or sound effects enhanced the presentation.
	Hyperlinks and/or navigation buttons did not function as expected.	Some of the hyperlinks and/or navigation may not have functioned appropriately.	Most hyperlinks and/or navigation functioned appropriately.	All hyperlinks and navigation functioned appropriately.
	A limited amount of notes in the "notes" section of Normal View were provided or were missing altogether.	Adequate notes in the "notes" section of Normal View were provided and were used to expand on the "talking points" in the presentation.	Required notes in the "notes" section of Normal View were provided and were used to expand somewhat on the "talking points" in the presentation.	Detailed notes in the "notes" section of Normal View were provided and were used to expand on the "talking points" in the presentation.
	Presenter read word for word from notes and/or from the presentation and/or made minimal eye contact with audience.	Presenter did not read word for word from notes nor from the presentation. Occasional eye contact with audience was established.	Presenter made eye contact with audience with only minimal use of notes.	Presenter made eye contact with and spoke to audience knowledgeably, referring to notes on occasion.
References	No references were given or were improperly cited.	References were included but may or may not have been properly cited using APA style.	A minimum of five sources were cited using APA style, with only minor errors.	A minimum of five sources were appropriately cited using APA style.
		Fewer than five sources supported the presentation, with at least one peer-reviewed journal article.	References clearly supported the presentation and included at least one peer-reviewed journal article.	References clearly supported the presentation and included at least one peer-reviewed journal article.

Chapter Five

Learning and Teaching

INTRODUCTION

The ultimate instructional leader of any school is the principal. Together with administrative colleagues (assistant principals, school-based instructional leaders, etc), a learning environment is created in which the school or school system's curriculum is presented in creative, interesting ways that allow the students to learn important concepts and demonstrate that learning by accomplishing appropriate tasks. In such a dynamic environment, the students are regularly assessed to see that learning is taking place and that instructional plans are evaluated and adapted to best meet the instructional needs of the students. This cyclical process manifests itself every day in the classroom with the lessons that the teacher prepares and presents to students. Technology is an incredibly powerful tool that can have a profound effect on student learning when integrated into daily lessons to support instruction in the content area.

The National Technology Standard that promotes a dynamic, digital-age learning culture is Standard II. Educational Administrators:

a. ensure instructional innovation focused on continuous improvement of digital-age learning
b. model and promote the frequent and effective use of technology for learning
c. provide learner-centered environments equipped with technology and learning resources to meet the individual, diverse needs of all learners
d. ensure effective practice in the study of technology and its infusion across the curriculum
e. promote and participate in local, national, and global learning communities that stimulate innovation, creativity, and digital-age collaboration

Activities in the Chapter include:

1. A technology-enriched lesson plan
2. A presentation of the lesson plan to grade-level faculty or departmental faculty
3. Evaluation of the lesson plan by the grade-level or departmental faculty members with the use of "Observation Look-Fors."

4. A summary and reflection on the comments from the "Observation Look-Fors" and recommendations for lesson improvement the next time it is presented

ACTIVITIES

1. Technology Enriched Lesson Plan Preliminary Preparation

a. Among other roles that administrators play, that of instructional leader is an essential one. In that role, you will be expected to provide guidance regarding lesson implementation. As an advocate for 21st century skill acquisition, you will also be called upon to provide leadership in the teaching of content that is supported or enhanced by the use of technology. As preparation for that role, you will develop a lesson that integrates technology. To begin that process, consider lessons you have taught in the past for the content for which you are certified. Examine lesson plans that you have already presented and identify ways various technological components might have been integrated in these lessons. In the case where a computer lab is not available, consider a teacher-guided exploration of a website that relates to the content being taught. In a lab setting, where there is a computer available for each student, you may provide a list of teacher-evaluated websites for student investigation. Use the evaluative criteria found at http://www.library.cornell.edu/olinuris/ref/webcrit.html from Chapter 3's Search Log to determine appropriateness of such sites. The use of existing Webquests or one that is teacher-created represents this type of technology, in which student inquiry takes center stage. For information on Webquests, you may want to visit Bernie Dodge's website, http://webquest.org. For lesson plan ideas, you might choose to visit Kathy Schrock's Guide for Educators at http://school.discoveryeducation.com/schrockguide/.

b. Identify a content area topic for which you would like to create a technology-enriched lesson. This can be a "real-world" situation that you will actually use in your current classroom. Or, it may be a lesson you would like to use in the future. If you are not currently placed in a teacher-level position, think of a lesson you could use in a classroom setting with which you are familiar. Or, visit a nearby school and discover what opportunities might exist there for a technology-enriched lesson.

c. Before you actually begin writing your plan, take a look at the national and state technology standards for students. Remember, every teacher should be teaching these standards in addition to their subject-specific curricular standards as they integrate technology into those subject-specific lessons. Every teacher is a technology teacher! And remember, integrating technology means that you are teaching your content using technology as a tool to assist in that process. It does not mean, "Today, we're going to have a technology lesson." This distinction is an important one. Refer to national or state technology standards. To assist you, you will find National and Maryland technology standards for students at:

   National Educational Technology Standards for Students (NETS-S 2007) http://www.iste.org/Content/NavigationMenu/NETS/ForStudents/2007Standards/NETS_for_Students_2007_Standards.pdf

When you have decided on the technology tools that will support your instruction, identify which of the technology standards are addressed by your lesson.

d. If you would like to see some examples of technology-enriched lessons, you may go to any of the sites listed below or to any of the hundreds of others that exist. An excellent example of the way technology has improved communication is how easy it is for educators to share ideas and entire lesson plans via the Internet. Remember that lesson plans found on the Internet often are not reviewed for accuracy or for sound instructional strategies. Carefully consider the requirements and guidelines of your school system before using a lesson plan from the Internet.

The School Improvement in Maryland site at http://mdk12.org/instruction/index.html

Verizon Thinkfinity (formerly Marco Polo) at http://www.marcopolo-education.org

Thinkport (co-created by Johns Hopkins University Center for Technology in Education and Maryland Public Television) at http://www.thinkport.org

Table 5.1. Technology Enriched Lesson Plan Proposal for a One-Day Lesson

GRADE LEVEL	LENGTH (in minutes) of one instructional class period
LESSON TOPIC	
State the new learning for students or the lesson objective	
Specific technology to be used by the teacher to support the lesson:	
Specific technology to be used by the students to support the lesson	
If students are using technology, what would be provided to students to help them acquire the necessary skills and when would they acquire them?	
Anticipated student product to be assessed (should demonstrate degree to which student has met the lesson objective)	

Kathy Schrock's Guide for Educators at http://school.discoveryeducation.com./schrockguide/

e. As you consider the lesson plan you will create, use the Technology Enriched Lesson Plan Proposal for a one-day technology-enriched lesson. This will allow you to consider critical lesson elements to ensure that you are moving in the right direction.

f. Now, begin writing your own lesson plan. You are not discouraged from using a lesson you have previously taught but in which you did not use technological tools. This may help you see:

- how much more effective your lesson might have been had you effectively integrated technology as an educational tool
- how easy it is to integrate technology in your content area

Be certain that your new plan meets all of the technology enriched lesson plan project specifications as described below:

- The subject, grade, and ability level of the class being taught (*e.g.*, Eleventh Grade Honors Physics)
- The title of the unit of instruction (*e.g.*, Acceleration and Velocity)
- The lesson's title (*e.g.*, "Using Technology to Investigate the Laws of Inertia")
- The NETS-S (National Educational Technology Standards for Students) indicators that will be addressed in your lesson
- Materials needed
- At least one objective in the "to do/to learn" format *(e.g.*, By the end of this lesson, students will be able to identify and apply Newton's laws of inertia by participating in an online inertia simulation.)
- A mind-jog, warm-up, or anticipatory set to get the students focused on the lesson content
- Detailed lesson procedures

  A specific, step-by-step description of how the lesson will unfold so that a similarly qualified teacher could conduct the lesson as you envision it

- A summary or closure (may be connected to the lesson's assessment)

  A student-created product or exit ticket (brief assessment of the lesson objective) designed to assess each individual student and inform the teacher as to what degree the students met the objective

- A scoring tool for the student-created product or for the assessment conducted at the end of the lesson (exit ticket)
- Differentiation strategies that would address learning styles and/or students with special needs
- A copy of at least one handout that the students will receive (and answer keys, if applicable)

In addition, your lesson plan must not violate any legal, social, or ethical uses of technology, including copyright laws. It should promote higher-level thinking skills, be student-centered, have a real-world context for learning the topic, and should be appropriate for the age/grade level of the students. The technology that is used in the lesson must genuinely enhance the instruction, yet the focus should be more on content than on learning how to use the technology.

As you prepare your lesson, you should use the lesson plan format required by your school or school system. If your required plan format does not include all of the items included on the previous page, please be sure to add those components to your lesson plan format. If you are new to teaching and are not sure exactly what a lesson plan format is, you could use the format in Table 5.2.

2. Lesson Presentation

Peer review and support is something we are fortunate to have easy access to as educators. Often, more than in other professions, educators seem to be willing to collaborate to share ideas, projects, and previous work they have done. Present your lesson to at least four of your departmental or grade-level colleagues with whom you teach or to fellow classmates from the course in which you are currently enrolled. Using Table 5.3 Technology Enriched Lesson Plan Peer Feedback, modeled after a document from the Baltimore County Public Schools Office of Instructional Technology, grade-level colleagues or fellow classmates should evaluate your lesson. While those using this form normally would be observing a technology teacher's lesson in an actual classroom, if the instructional procedures are sufficiently detailed, it will be relatively easy to use this tool to evaluate a technology-enriched lesson simply by reading it and/or having it described in a small group setting. Remember, it is important to note that not every lesson will address all of the bulleted items on the Technology Enriched Lesson Plan Peer Feedback form.

3. Summary of Peer Feedback (final item in the Technology Enriched Lesson Plan Format)

Review your colleagues' comments on your technology enriched lesson. Summarize the strengths they perceived in your lesson. Identify the recommendations for lesson improvement and outline the potential modifications you will make in this lesson. Include in the Evaluation of Your Lesson section of your lesson plan, a summary of the peer feedback and your reflection on that feedback.

Table 5.2. Technology Enriched Lesson Plan Format

Name:
Subject or Content Area:
Grade Level/Ability Level:
Title of Unit/Title of Lesson:
Lesson Objective: The student will be able to....by....
Academic Standards and Performance Indicators: *(Refer to content standards for your content area)*
Technology Standards and Performance Indicators National Educational Technology Standards for Students (NETS-S) http://www.iste.org/Content/NavigationMenu/NETS/ForStudents/2007Standards/NETS_for_Students_2007_Standards.pdf
Equipment/Materials: List all items necessary for the lesson.

(continued)

Table 5.2. (*continued*)

Online Resources:

Instructional Procedures
List your procedures step by step so that another teacher could accomplish your lesson as you envision it. Include a warm up or drill (motivation), transitions between the learner-centered activities, modifications for differentiation, discussion questions used in the lesson, lesson closure, and the assessment of the lesson objective.

Student Evaluation
Include an assessment that students complete or the creation of a student product/performance to demonstrate their progress in meeting this lesson's objective. Provide the scoring tool.

Follow Up
Identify homework or other activities that will serve as follow-up to the lesson.

Your Evaluation of the Lesson
Include a summary of the peer feedback you received from colleagues and your reflection on that feedback.

Table 5.3. Technology Enriched Lesson Plan Peer Feedback

Category	Description
Initial Reflection *Note: These questions can be used in the pre-observation conference.*	*It is evident that the teacher has considered the following questions when planning the technology integrated lesson:* ☐ Is the technology appropriate for this lesson? Why? Why not? ☐ What technology skills do my students already have that are needed for this lesson? ☐ What technology skills will they need to learn to complete this lesson successfully? ☐ How will I embed the technology skills instruction into my lesson? ☐ How much time can I allow for this lesson? Can this lesson be successfully completed in this amount of time?
General	☐ Technology adds value to the lesson. Some learning activities would not be possible without technology. Technology use maximizes active student involvement in the lesson. ☐ The lesson models legal and ethical uses of technology. ☐ The lesson is aligned to the curriculum. ☐ All components of a good lesson are present. ☐ There is evidence of collaboration with other teachers (co-teaching or collaborative planning).
Standards	☐ The lesson is aligned to content and technology standards. ☐ The content is the focus of the lesson, not the hardware or software applications being used. ☐ The use of technology is appropriate for the grade level.
Assessment	☐ Assessment expectations are communicated to students in advance. ☐ The scoring tool addresses both content and technology. ☐ Learning reflects the effective use of technology (e.g., student products, evidence of use of technology during implementation of the lesson).
Resources	☐ Content resources are listed. ☐ Hardware resources are listed and are appropriate for the grade level. ☐ Software resources are listed and are appropriate for the grade level.

(continued)

Table 5.3. (*continued*)

Implementation	❑ Varied instructional strategies are employed (visual, auditory, kinesthetic, tactile). ❑ The lesson is well structured to maximize time on task. ❑ The lesson has an appropriate motivational activity. ❑ Students are engaged. ❑ The lesson progresses logically through well planned procedures. ❑ Transitions between activities help to maintain lesson flow. ❑ An appropriate assessment, which addresses both content and technology, is present. ❑ The lesson has a closing activity/summary.
Management Strategies	❑ There is an established routine for how students will enter, exit, and move about as they work in the technology lab/classroom. ❑ Students sit in assigned seats. ❑ Behavior management strategies ensure students are engaged and learning. ❑ There is a predetermined method for how students should obtain teacher attention. ❑ There is a predetermined method for how teacher will obtain student attention. ❑ There are established routines/strategies to manage how and when students will print work. ❑ There is back up plan for technology that fails.
Differentiation/ Accessibility	❑ A variety of student groupings are employed. ❑ Teacher makes learning accessible for all students. ❑ Instruction is differentiated for content, process, or product. ❑ Instruction is differentiated for students at various skill levels.
Final Reflection *Note: These questions can be used in the post-observation conference.*	*It is evident that the teacher has considered the following questions after implementing the technology integrated lesson:* ❑ To what extent did the students achieve the content objective(s)? How do you know? ❑ To what extent did the students achieve the technology indicator? How do you know? ❑ Was the scoring tool you developed an effective way to assess student technology skills? If so, how? If not, why? ❑ What will you do differently next time to ensure success for all students? ❑ In what ways was this lesson more effective because technology was used?

Table 5.4. Technology Enriched Lesson Plan Scoring Tool

Criterion	Unacceptable (1)	Acceptable (2)	Competent (3)	Exemplary (4)
Comprehensive Assessment of Lesson Plan	The lesson plan lacks understandable details. The purpose, procedure, task, resources, and evaluation are not defined and/or parts are missing. Other teachers would have a hard time reproducing this plan. Guiding questions are not appropriate for topic and/or inadequate.	The lesson plan somewhat describes the task, resources and evaluation. With modification, other teachers can use the plan. Guiding questions are appropriate for topic but do not promote higher-level thinking skills.	The lesson plan lists the procedure, task, resources, and evaluation process. They are adequately defined. Other teachers could use the plan. Guiding questions are appropriate for topic and promote some higher-level thinking skills.	The lesson plan explains the purpose, procedure, task, resources, and evaluation process. All are clearly defined and can be easily reproduced by other teachers. Guiding questions are appropriate for topic and promote many higher-level thinking skills.
Content Standards and Objectives	The lesson plan is not related to current state or school curriculum standards. The lesson plan does not include learning expectations and/or performance indicators.	The lesson plan is based on current state or school curriculum standards or competencies. Learning expectations and/or performance indicators are not listed in sufficient detail.	The lesson plan is based on current state or school curriculum standards or competencies. Learning expectations are adequately noted. Performance indicators are listed and the plan shows how they are measured.	The lesson plan is based on current state or school curriculum standards or competencies. It establishes specific learning expectations. Performance indicators are clearly defined and are easily measured.
Procedures and Learning Activities	Teacher preparation and timeline is poorly or inadequately explained. Students are exposed to trivial learning activities. The plan shows no development of students using higher-level thinking skills.	The plan identifies some teacher preparation and timeline details. Students experience at least one or more learning activities. The plan shows some development of students using higher-level thinking skills.	The plan lists teacher preparation and timeline specifics. Students are exposed to a variety of learning activities. The plan shows how students can use higher-level thinking skills as they work.	The plan clearly defines the teacher preparation and timeline. Learning activities are student-centered, collaborative, and promote learning. The plan specifically identifies how students will use higher-level thinking skills in the activities.

(continued)

Table 5.4. (continued)

Criterion	Unacceptable (1)	Acceptable (2)	Competent (3)	Exemplary (4)
Integration of Technology, Including Websites	Using technology does little to enhance student learning in this lesson. Few technology concepts are used in this lesson and they are not authentic. Students are not actively engaged in learning with technology.	Students use technology in this lesson as a supplement to learning. There is little evidence of direct instruction for students on the target technology(ies). There is some evidence it enhances learning goals but it is not necessarily authentic. Efforts to engage students in using technology tools meet minimal requirements.	Technology is used to encourage student learning in this lesson plan. Students use one or more technology tools for authentic learning. Lesson includes sufficient direct instruction or evidence of prior instruction for students on the appropriate use of the target technology(ies). Technology is used by students to acquire knowledge and/or demonstrate learning.	It is evident technology is used to enhance student learning and is aligned with the purpose of the lesson. Multiple technologies are used for authentic learning. Lesson includes direct instruction or evidence of prior instruction for students on the appropriate use of the target technology(ies) in order to ensure student success. Students are guided into project-based learning where technology is used as a tool. The use of technology in this lesson inspires extended learning.
Student Product	The student product is shows little or no real world application of the content and the technology. The context of the student product is missing entirely. A real or simulated audience for the product may is not identified.	The student product is limited in its real world application of the content and the technology. The context of the student product is either poorly established or is missing entirely. A real or simulated audience for the product may or may not be identified.	The student product somewhat reflects a real world application of the content and the technology. The context of the student product is established although it may not be clear to students that it is designed for a real or simulated audience.	The student product reflects a real world application of the content and the technology. The context of the student product is well-developed and it is clear to students that it is designed for a real or simulated audience.

Criterion	Unacceptable (1)	Acceptable (2)	Competent (3)	Exemplary (4)
Student Assessment	Assessment criteria for this technology lesson are absent or not clearly identified. Assessment is not aligned with curriculum standards or performance criteria.	An adequate assessment exists to evaluate student learning but no evidence exists showing it is conveyed to students. Evaluation criteria somewhat address the objectives of the lesson and the developmental level of the students.	An assessment to evaluate student learning is developed and is conveyed to students. The assessment employs evaluative criteria appropriate to objectives and the developmental level of the students and includes use of technology.	An appropriate assessment is developed to appraise student learning and is conveyed to students. Assessment guidelines include evaluating the student's ability to use technology for problem solving and are appropriate for the subject matter
Feedback and Summary	A vague or no explanation of peer feedback is included. Reflective statement is missing or does not identify lesson's strengths or need for revisions.	A vague explanation of peer feedback is included. Reflective statement identifies some of the lesson's strengths and areas of possible revisions.	A somewhat clear explanation of peer feedback is included. Reflective statement identifies some of the lesson's strengths and areas of possible revisions.	A very clear explanation of peer feedback is included. Reflective statement identifies many of the lesson's strengths and areas of possible revisions.

Index

Administrators: role, 1, 7–8, 34, 46, 54
Assignment templates, electronic versions, xii

Budget, 4; narrative scoring tool, 4; technology, 3

Copyright. *See* Social, legal, ethical issues

Data: analysis of, 13–14; data-driven instructional decisions, 13–14; use of, 7–8

English Language Learners (ELLs), 9, 12
Excel® spreadsheet, 8–12, 15

Faculty Professional Growth: activity, 15; checklist, 8, 22–23, 26; Professional Development Outline, 20; scoring tool, 32–33; timeline, 8, 26–27, 29–30

Grade Book, Class, 8–12

Interview, budget: administrator in charge of budget, 3; administrator in charge of facilities, 3; scoring tool, 5; technology coordinator, 3
Individual Educational Plan (IEP), 9, 12
International Society for Technology in Education, xi
ISTE. *See* International Society for Technology in Education

Lesson plan, technology-enriched, 54; format, 59–60; peer feedback, 58, 61–62; proposal template, 56; samples, 56; scoring tool, 63–65; specifications, 57

Microsoft Office®, xii

National Educational Technology Standards for Administrators. *See* Standards, NETS-A
NETS-A Standards. *See* Standards NETS-A

PowerPoint®, 6–7, 12; Social, Legal, Ethical presentation, 47–48, 62–64. *See also* Social, Legal, Ethical issues
Professional Development Outline, 20; scoring tool, 21

School Improvement Plan goals, 8, 13
Scoring tools, xii; Case Study and Observation/Reflection, 43; Faculty Technology and Professional Growth Plan Technology and Timeline Advocacy Potential, 32; Social, Legal, Ethical Issues Search Log, 37; Social, Legal, Ethical Uses of Technology presentation, 52; Technology-Enriched Lesson Plan, 63; Technology Interviews and Budget Narrative, 5; Using Data Professional Development Outline, 21; Using Data to Improve Student Achievement, 16

Social, legal, ethical issues, 34–37, 46, 52–53; Case Study and Observation/Reflection activity, 39–42; Case Study and Observation/Reflection scoring tool, 43–45; informal case studies, 38; search log, 34–37; scoring tool, search log, 37; scoring tool, PowerPoint® presentation, 64

Software: administrative, 3; instructional, 3

Standards, ISTE, ix, xi; NETS-A: Standard I, indicators, 25–26; Standard II, indicators, 54; Standard III, indicators, 46; Standard IV, indicators, 2; Standard V, indicators, 34; Technology, for students, 55

Student achievement, using data to improve, 8; scoring tool, 16–19

Systems improvement: strategies, 7

Technology standards. *See* Standards, NETS-A

Technology systems: evaluation of, 4; improvement, 4, 7; Technology advocacy, 28, 31

Templates, electronic versions, xii

Websites, criteria for evaluation of, 36, 55

www.ingramcontent.com/pod-product-compliance
Lightning Source LLC
Chambersburg PA
CBHW081834300426
44116CB00014B/2590